IAN McALLISTER & NICHOLAS READ

THE SEA WOLVES

LIVING WILD IN THE GREAT BEAR RAINFOREST

PHOTOGRAPHS BY IAN McALLISTER

ORCA BOOK PUBLISHERS

Library and Archives Canada Cataloguing in Publication

McAllister, Ian, 1969-
The sea wolves : living wild in the Great Bear
Rainforest / written by Ian McAllister and Nicholas
Read ; photographs by Ian McAllister.

Issued also in electronic format.
ISBN 978-1-55469-206-4

1. Wolves--British Columbia--Great Bear Rainforest--Juvenile
literature. 2. Rain forest ecology--British Columbia--Juvenile
literature. 3. Great Bear Rainforest (B.C.)--Juvenile literature.

I. Read, Nicholas, 1956- II. Title.
QL737.C22M324 2010   J599.773'097111   C2010-903534-8

First published in the United States, 2010
Library of Congress Control Number: 2010928820

Summary: The coastal wolf, a genetically distinct strain that swims and fishes, inhabits the Great Bear Rainforest
on British Columbia's rugged west coast.

Mixed Sources
Cert no. SW-COC-001271
© 1996 FSC
FSC

*Orca Book Publishers is dedicated to preserving the environment and has printed this book
on paper certified by the Forest Stewardship Council.*

Orca Book Publishers gratefully acknowledges the support for its publishing programs provided by the
following agencies: the Government of Canada through the Canada Book Fund and the Canada Council for the Arts,
and the Province of British Columbia through the BC Arts Council and the Book Publishing Tax Credit.

Design by Teresa Bubela
Layout by Nadja Penaluna
Cover and interior images by Ian McAllister
Page v map by D. Leversee, Sierra Club BC
Photo of Ian McAllister by Douglas Cowell
Photo of Nicholas Read by Dave Scougal

About the photographs:
All of the images in this book are of wild animals in wild circumstances.
No digital manipulation or other alterations have taken place.

ORCA BOOK PUBLISHERS
PO Box 5626, Stn. B
VICTORIA, BC Canada
V8R 6S4

ORCA BOOK PUBLISHERS
PO Box 468
CUSTER, WA USA
98240-0468

www.orcabook.com
Printed and bound in Canada.

13 12 11 10 • 4 3 2 1

RIGHT: **Coastal wolves are
excellent swimmers and
can easily cross several
kilometers of open ocean.**

CONTENTS

LEFT: **Canada's Great Bear Rainforest is a spectacular wilderness of towering trees and salmon-filled rivers.**

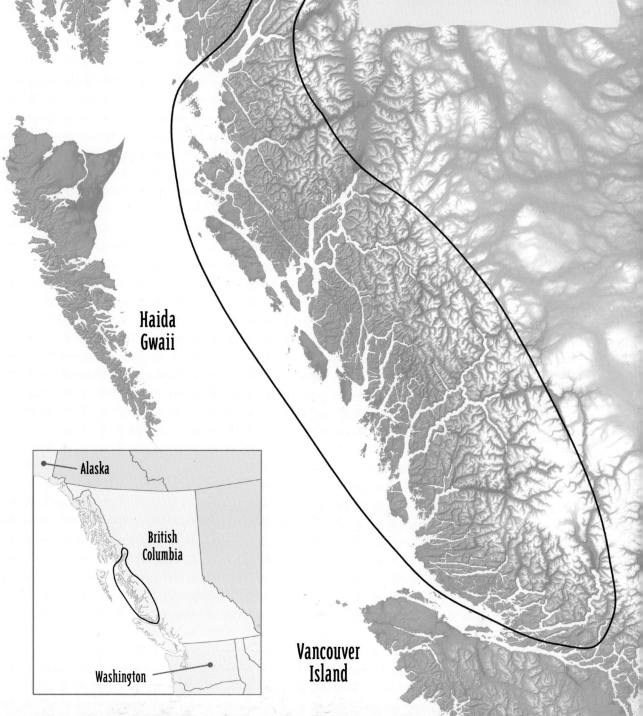

Great Bear Rainforest
British Columbia

Haida
Gwaii

Vancouver
Island

Alaska

British
Columbia

Washington

CHAPTER ONE

A Bad Rap

"Who's afraid of the big bad wolf, the big bad wolf, the big bad wolf? Who's afraid of the big bad wolf? Tra la la la la." You may remember this song from when you were younger. The Three Little Pigs sang it in a Disney cartoon made way back in 1933. (You can still see it on YouTube.) In the cartoon, the wolf, who walks upright on his hind legs and wears an Abe Lincoln stovepipe hat and hillbilly britches, blows down one little pig's house made of straw and another made of sticks. But he can't blow down the third pig's house because it's made of bricks. So he scrambles up to the roof and climbs down the chimney only to be boiled alive in a cauldron of water in the fireplace. In the cartoon, the wolf manages to escape—his badly burned backside blowing a plume of smoke as he runs away. But in the original English

LEFT: **Wolves, like this young subadult, are curious, intelligent and among the most social animals on the planet.**

WOLF BITES

How are wolves and people alike?

Both are very social and very affectionate with their young. Both live in hierarchical societies (meaning someone's the boss) and family groups. Wolves have alpha leaders who are like the parents of the pack. Both wolves and people are also very chatty. People love to talk, and so do wolves. They will bark, yelp, whine, whimper, growl, howl and squeak in different ways and at different volumes to let other wolves know what's on their minds. Also like humans, wolves are very territorial and willing to defend those territories to the death. Think of how many wars humans have fought over precisely the same thing.

RIGHT: **Two siblings share an affectionate moment in some tall grass. One of these young wolves may become the leader of his pack one day, but that will depend on leadership skills and whether he wants the job.**

version of the story, written more than half a century earlier, he isn't so lucky. The pig who built the brick house covers the pot and cooks the wolf for supper.

Regardless of which version of "The Three Little Pigs" you encounter, the message of the story is clear: wolves are big, bad and dangerous—to people and pigs—and the only good one is a dead one. It's a view many people have held for centuries. Think of the folktales you know in which wolves play a part. Then think about the parts those wolves play.

In "Little Red Riding Hood," a German fairy tale also filmed by Disney, a wolf eats a little girl's grandmother and then the girl herself. They're saved, however, when a hunter cuts the wolf open and finds the little girl and her grandmother alive and whole inside. The wolf also plays the villain in "Peter and the Wolf," a Russian story in which a young boy's pet duck is caught and eaten by—what else?—a wolf. Then, just as in "Little Red Riding Hood," hunters capture the wolf, tie him up and take him to a zoo in a victory parade led by the boy, Peter. At the end, the storyteller says if you listen carefully you can still hear the duck quacking because the wolf, in his greed and haste for a meal, swallowed her alive.

But our fear and loathing of wolves doesn't end there. It shows up in sayings too. When we run short of money, we say "the wolf is at the door," as if having a wolf at our door would be the very worst thing that could happen to us. When someone is described as being "a wolf in sheep's clothing," it means he or she is really no good and is only pretending to be gentle and kind. When we "cry wolf," it means we're

WOLF BITES

Wolves in history.

The city of Rome is said to have been founded by Romulus and Remus, both sons of Mars, the Roman god of war, who were suckled as babies by a she-wolf. Because of this, Romans believed it was lucky to see a wolf. Julius Caesar's victory over the Gauls in 195 BC was attributed to a wolf sent by Mars to frighten the enemy. Some ancient Europeans believed that when wolves howled, it was really the spirits of the dead calling to the living. The werewolf, which is half man and half wolf, was a monster made popular by Hollywood in the 1930s, but the idea probably came from the medieval practice of people dressing up as wolves. On BC's central coast, the Heiltsuk First Nation believes people belonging to the wolf clan are elevated in stature in times of war or famine, and that wolves are protectors and providers of their nation. The Cree, a First Nations people who live in large parts of eastern Canada and the US, tell a story somewhat like that of Noah's Ark. They believe that after the Great Flood, a wolf pushed a ball of absorbent moss round and round the survivors' raft until the Earth was reformed.

lying about, or exaggerating, a situation and will be punished for it.

With so many messages around about wolves being sly, unpredictable, vicious and bloodthirsty, is it any wonder that, even in a modern, scientific and environmentally aware society such as ours, people still regard them as enemies? Or worse, as vermin—something to get rid of?

If you doubt that, consider that it wasn't long ago that wolves could be found throughout most of North America. Not anymore. Outside of Alaska they have been ruthlessly exterminated from 95 percent of the places they used to live in the United States. The US government hated them so much that for over a hundred years it paid a *bounty*, a reward of money, to whoever killed a wolf anywhere in the country. The same thing happened in Canada. One of the first acts of the new government of Upper Canada—what is now Ontario—was to offer a cash payment to anyone who would rid the country of its wolves. Yet to this day there has not been a single documented case of a person in North America being killed by a wolf. (In 2005, a university student working in a mining camp in northern Saskatchewan was found dead with wolves observed nearby, but it has never been determined whether he was killed by wolves or a bear.)

Thankfully, wolves are still present in parts of North America. In Canada, which has far fewer people than the United States and therefore more room for wildlife, they can be found in most provinces except for parts of the Prairies and Maritimes. In British

Columbia, where the wolves featured in this book live, they're found almost everywhere except Haida Gwaii, a chain of islands off the province's northwest coast. But even today they are under constant threat. In BC there are no real restrictions against killing them. You need a special license to hunt deer, ducks, geese, bear, moose and elk in BC. And when you kill a bear or an elk, you have to report when and where you made the kill. Not so with wolves. Officially you're allowed to kill three a year, but if you do, you don't have to tell anyone about it, which makes it almost impossible for anyone, including scientists, to understand the full impact hunting has on wolves.

That's why we thought it was time a different kind of book told a different kind of story about wolves.

TOP: **A black wolf searches for salmon on a bright fall day. Rainforest wolves come in different colors—ranging from black to white—but the most common color is brown with reddish highlights.**

5

Because if you put aside all the bad press they've received in North American history, European fairy tales and Disney cartoons, and you take the time to learn what they're really like, you'll discover that wolves are fascinating. And that the fishing, swimming wolves who live in the rainforest along BC's central and northern coast are especially so. Yes, like all wolves, they eat other animals to live. Wolves are carnivores, meaning they need to hunt other animals to survive. And that's not always a pretty sight. But people eat other animals too, and that isn't pretty either. In fact, and as this book will make clear, wolves and people aren't as different as you might think. For example, like people, wolves are very social. They live in packs that are really extended families. They also have jobs, play and take care of their young, whom

BOTTOM: **These two wolves belong to a pack conservationists have called the Fish Trap pack because it lives near an ancient First Nations fishing spot. They feed on salmon between September and November.**

they value more than anything. In these and other ways, wolves are a lot more like humans—like you and your friends—than people realize. Could this be one of the reasons people are so hard on them? Perhaps when we see things in wolves we don't like, we're reminded of things we don't like about ourselves.

The wolves who live in this coastal rainforest represent one of the last populations of wolves on Earth that are able to teach us what wolves are really like because they're also one of the last wolf populations that hasn't been affected in a big way by human contact. So as you read this book, we hope you'll come to understand that wolves, and particularly the wolves living along BC's central coast, are anything but the monsters of myth. Rather, we hope you'll come to regard them as remarkable, social, intelligent creatures—creatures who play a vital role in maintaining

TOP: **Wolves live in extended families called packs. Each pack is led by one male and one female, who also act as the breeding pair. Next to that of primates, the social structure of a wolf family is one of the most complex and evolved in the animal world.**

7

WOLF BITES

Wolves in the Christian tradition.

Some early Christians believed the wolf was the earthly incarnation of Satan, so they wanted all wolves killed to rid people of sin. But some Christian saints, including Saint Francis of Assisi, are said to have tamed wolves. Saint Austreberthe, an abbot who lived in medieval France, had a donkey that was killed by a wolf. So he made the wolf carry his water bucket instead.

RIGHT: **This wolf is just growing his new coat in preparation for a long, dark and wet winter. Because of the relatively mild climate on the BC coast, rainforest wolves grow a thick winter coat for only a short period of time.**

the health of one of the last great wildernesses on Earth. And for that reason they deserve our respect much more than our fear.

It's certainly true that wolves are efficient hunters. So if you're ever in a part of the forest where wolves live, you have to be wary of them. But wolves also demonstrate many other characteristics—characteristics people must have recognized and admired long ago. Why? Because it was from the wild wolf that the domestic dog was born 12,000 to 14,000 years ago. That's right, without the wolf we never would have been introduced to "man's best friend." Whoever took in the first wild wolf and made him or her a companion to be loved, not feared, must have recognized a certain kinship between people and wolves. Those people must have seen how much wolves enjoyed being with other wolves, just as today's dogs enjoy being with other dogs and people. Of course, many of the dogs we live with today look nothing like wolves. That's thanks to years of careful and selective breeding. At the same time there are other breeds, like the German shepherd, the husky and the malamute, where the resemblance is as plain as the snouts on their faces. But even though the cockapoo or labradoodle might not look it, they have some wolf in them too. Why do you think dog trainers sometimes refer to domestic dogs as "the wolf in your living room"?

The wolves we're talking about in this book are from a unique population living along the west coast of British Columbia in an area known as the Great Bear Rainforest. This area got its name because

of the great bears—the American blacks, grizzlies and spirit bears (a black bear with white fur)—who live there too. But it would be a mistake to think that the rainforest, which extends from the top of Vancouver Island to the tip of Alaska's Panhandle and inward from the Pacific Ocean to the Coast Mountains, is home to nothing but bears. Hundreds of other animals—moose, cougars, mountain goats, deer, whales, seals, sea lions, toads, reptiles, myriad birds, and who knows how many different kinds of insects—live there too.

So do wolves. But these wolves are different from their inland cousins; these wolves can swim like otters and fish like bears. They're called coastal wolves because they live near the sea. For aboriginal, or First Nations, people who have shared the land with them for generations, they're as much a part of the land- and seascape as the grizzly, the salmon and the killer whale. But it's only recently that scientists have come to understand their uniqueness: that they

WOLF BITES

Fish in the northwest Pacific.

Pacific halibut, Pacific cod, lingcod, black cod, five species of Pacific salmon, five species of sole, Pacific pollock, herring, perch and hagfish are some of the many kinds of fish that populate the vast and deep waters off the coast of the Great Bear Rainforest.

LEFT: **This yawning wolf pup shows the size of its jaws and why wolves are such efficient hunters. An adult wolf can bite a deer leg in half with its powerful mouth. Its jaw is more than twice as powerful as that of a domestic dog.**

RIGHT: **The Great Bear Rainforest is full of black bears, but they have to be on guard all the time because wolves may attack them. Even adult bears may be hunted by wolves.**

WOLF BITES

How many teeth does a wolf have?

Adult gray and red wolves have 42 highly specialized teeth, compared to humans who have 32. A wolf's canine teeth, or fangs, can be 6.5 centimeters (2.5 inches) long and are used for gripping and puncturing the flesh of their prey. Other sets of teeth are used for nipping small pieces of meat, tearing flesh away from bones, and grinding and crushing bones and flesh. A wolf's jaw is so strong that it can sever the hind leg of a moose in just six to eight bites.

RIGHT: **This wolf has a porcupine quill lodged in his nose—the painful consequence of trying to hunt the sharp-quilled creature. There are risks attached to hunting just about any animal, and wolves have to weigh these every time they head off in search of prey.**

are genetically distinct from wolves in the interior of British Columbia, and different from any other wolf in any other part of the world.

One of the differences between coastal wolves and wolves on the other side of the Coast Range, a spine of mountains that runs along the western edge of British Columbia, is that they're smaller. In fact, they are about 20 percent smaller. That makes them roughly the size of a long-legged German shepherd dog. Why the difference? Science's best guess is that warmer temperatures on the coast mean the wolves who live there don't have to grow larger. A general rule of nature is the colder the environment, the larger the animal. Why? Think about it: skinny people tend to get cold faster than heavyset people because they carry less "padding." Or put another way, heavyset people pack a lot more insulation. The same is true of wildlife. This probably explains why polar bears in the Arctic and tigers in Siberia grow much larger than bears and tigers in warmer places.

This notion of being only as big as you need to be prevails throughout nature. That's because nature, unlike the communities humans build, is a very energy-efficient place. Just as the fuel that heats your home or runs your car isn't limitless, neither is the energy in nature. It comes from the food animals and plants eat. And because there's only so much food to go around, nature has created ways for it to be used efficiently. One of these ways is for animals like wolves to grow no bigger than they have to.

Another difference between coastal and inland wolves is that the coastal wolf's fur is coarser and less

TOP: **Rainforest wolves are slightly smaller than their gray wolf cousins, who live in the far north and interior of North America. This pale brown wolf splashing his way through a river has just shed his winter coat, so he looks particularly thin.**

dense than his inland cousin's. This also makes sense from an energy-saving perspective because it doesn't get as cold on the coast as it does inland. So regardless of whether you're a wolf or a person, you don't need as thick a coat. And while inland wolves are mostly silver gray in color, many coastal wolves have a distinctive rust red hue. In fact, many are multicolored—they have ocher and sepia on their ears and back, and black and silver or white down their sides. But almost all of them have a special red tint all their own.

Another big difference between the two types of wolves is that coastal wolves swim—a lot. And if that surprises you, think of your dog. Certain breeds of dogs like Labradors and spaniels love swimming and are very good at it. Well, so are BC's coastal wolves.

Some have been known to swim distances as great as thirteen kilometers (eight miles). That's almost five times the length of the Golden Gate Bridge in San Francisco. The fact that these wolves are such good swimmers makes good sense. When you stop to think about it, that's true of almost everything in nature. Off the coast of the Great Bear Rainforest there are hundreds of big and small islands and many more lakes, rivers, streams, bays and inlets. Surrounded by all this water, coastal wolves have to get around somehow. Boats aren't an option, so what else is there but swimming? They swim from island to island to find the deer, salmon and other animals they survive on. And if they find a seal, a beached whale or another kind of marine mammal along the way, they'll eat it too. When fall arrives, they also fish for salmon that swim up the rivers to spawn and die. An old Russian proverb says "The wolf is kept fed by his feet." In BC's coastal forest, their feet help them swim too.

But perhaps the most amazing thing about these coastal wolves is that for as long as they've been around, they've lived among people who not only don't hate them but actually value them. The people of the Great Bear Rainforest have never sought to hurt or punish wolves. Instead these First Nations people have always believed wolves have as much right to a place in the world as human beings. In most other places where wolves are found—from Russia to the Rockies—they've been persecuted by humans with a kind of madness. Not in the Great Bear Rainforest. The GBR is one place in the world where wolves have been allowed to live in

WOLF BITES

From wild wolf to pet dog.

It's now believed that pet dogs evolved from gray wolves living in the Middle East. Scientists used to think dogs came from East Asian wolves, but recent research says this isn't so. In 2010, researchers from California, Canada, Israel, China, Australia and Europe examined genetic material from more than 900 pet dogs, representing 85 different breeds. They compared this to DNA from more than 200 gray wolves from North America, Europe, the Middle East and East Asia. They found that gray wolves from the Middle East are genetically closer to pet dogs than any other kind of wolf. The Middle East is also where domestic cats and many kinds of livestock originated, and is where agriculture was developed. This is why it's often called "the cradle of civilization." Scientists say they know dogs from the Middle East have been associated with humans for thousands of years because bones from dogs have been found in ancient human graves. In one grave a puppy was found curled up in the arms of its human companion.

comparative harmony with humans. When European settlers came to British Columbia in the nineteenth and twentieth centuries, that began to change. But even then, because the Great Bear Rainforest is so difficult to get to and so far away from places where immigrants built their cities and towns, coastal wolves remained fairly well protected.

This book tells their story. It will explain that rather than the big, bad, grandmother-swallowing beasts of European folklore, the wolves of coastal British Columbia are creatures to cherish and admire. Yes, they are hunters, but that's how they fit into nature and help maintain her balance. Like the great bears who give the rainforest its name, the wolves are a magnificent rainforest symbol: brave, loyal, resourceful and clever. Creatures who deserve our care, our respect and our protection, just like any other natural treasure.

WOLF BITES

Are there any laws in BC that protect wild wolves from overt cruelty?

No. While animals in cities, such as cats and dogs, enjoy a small measure of protection against abuse, animals in the wild don't. Imagine the uproar if your pet dog was caught in a leghold trap. Well, wolves are caught in leghold traps all the time and hardly anyone bats an eye.

LEFT: **Coastal wolves in the Great Bear Rainforest are genetically distinct. This means their genetic makeup is different from other wolf populations, including other wolves living elsewhere in North America. They also look different from their inland cousins. They're slightly smaller, and they have more red in their coats.**

RIGHT: **The round pink objects in this wolf scat are evidence of salal berries in the wolf's diet. While wolves are dedicated carnivores, meaning they eat fish and meat for almost all their calories, they also will eat grass, berries and other foods on occasion.**

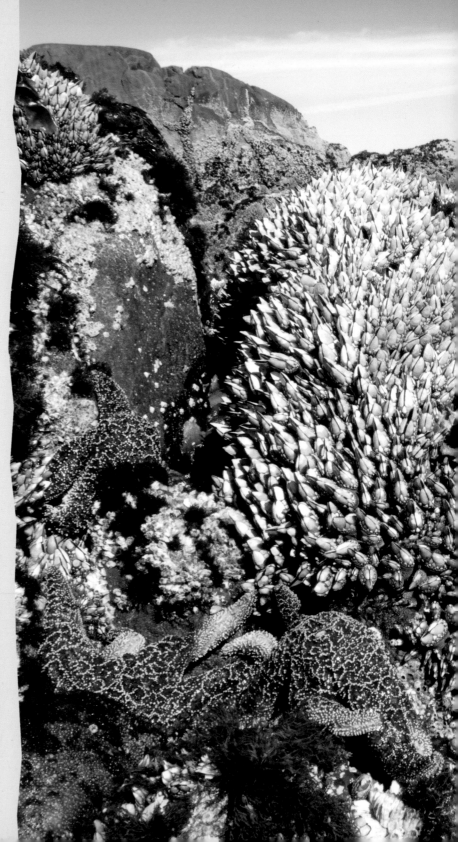

RIGHT: **The Great Bear Rainforest is defined as much by the sea as by the land, and coastal wolves are at home in both. When the tide goes out, an assortment of brightly colored marine life becomes visible along the rocky shoreline—marine life that wolves will eat. Wolves don't rely on crabs, barnacles and mussels for a big part of their diet, but when you're as hungry as a wolf, you'd be foolish to turn down an easy-to-catch meal.**

CHAPTER TWO

Babes in the Woods

Nature has her share of secrets—things humans rarely get to see. And the annual birth of the Great Bear Rainforest's new wolf pups is one of the best-kept secrets of all. But it's a ritual we're learning more about all the time. Imagine a cozy dry den dug under the roots of a massive old cedar tree. Inside, a proud mother wolf is lovingly suckling a litter of pups. The litter is large—five newborn wolves, each the size of a small loaf of bread and all squirming for more of the precious life-giving milk. Nursing five hungry pups isn't easy, but the past year was a good one. The deer were plentiful, so there was lots of food for the mother wolf and her rainforest family to eat. As a result, she, the highest-ranking female of the family, felt strong and healthy when she became

LEFT: **These moss-covered logs are all that's left of an old big house that once belonged to First Nations people on the coast. Coastal wolves and people have shared the same rainforest territories for thousands of years.**

WOLF BITES

The coastal wolf's beginnings.

No one knows for sure how the coastal wolf first came to the Great Bear Rainforest. Some scientists believe that as the last ice age receded, about 12,000 years ago, the wolves followed the deer population as it moved north into Canada from what is now the western United States. Others believe the islands along BC's coast could have been a refuge from the ice. They speculate that, unlike the continental mainland, parts of the coast were never covered in ice. If that's true, the coastal wolves could have lived through the last ice age feeding on the salmon and sea mammals—the seals and sea lions— that managed to survive these glaciation events too.

RIGHT: **These pups are about two months old and are just beginning to explore their rainforest home. Pups are usually born in litters of four to five in dens dug at the base of a large tree, where wolves can also dig dry and protected tunnels that help them hide from predators, like cougars and bears.**

pregnant two months ago. Because of this, her pups have a good chance of surviving to adulthood.

The den is dark, and the floor is packed hard and solid. To make it comfortable, members of the wolf pack have put down a quilt of cushiony materials they found close by—cedar bark, twigs, different kinds of grass and some dry moss. Thanks to these homey touches, the mother wolf has a soft bed to lie on. They were added especially for this year's birth, but the den itself is ancient. There's no telling how many genera- tions of wolves have used this same site. In fact, this particular mother wolf was born in the same den six years ago. Some wolf dens are hundreds of years old— as old as the once-grand family homes of Europe. But unlike some of those ruins, the den is still solid and comfortable—something the mother wolf who chose it again this year appreciates.

Outside it's quiet and dark. Some members of the wolf family, including the pups' father, the family's leader or alpha male, are sleeping in various locations scattered around the den site. Others are perched on a rocky outcropping under a big stand of cedar trees above the den, where they can keep a close watch on it and anything that comes near. Above them birds chatter, and in the distance are other rainforest sounds: the rumble of ocean waves crashing on the shore; the patter of rain on a pond; the whoosh of the coastal wind as it blows through stands of hemlock, cypress and yew trees. But the wolves are silent. No one howls because this is the wolves' quiet season. They don't want any harm to come to the pups, so they're careful not to bring any attention to what,

after all, is supposed to be a secret. Every strange noise, no matter how hushed, is noted and understood. If it's a sound the wolves haven't heard before, they investigate quickly. Nothing is taken for granted, because nothing is more precious to a wolf family than newborn pups. Just as in a human family, newborns are the wolf family's future, so everyone does his or her best to ensure their safety.

For the next three weeks or so, the pups will get all the nourishment they need from their mother's milk. They also won't move around much. Instead they'll remain in the den, hidden and protected, as they grow bigger, stronger, more confident and more independent. Their mother never leaves them. Instead the rest of the pack goes out and brings food back to her so she'll stay strong while she nurses her pups. During this time, the pups are happy to stay close to mom. But when those three weeks are up and they're big enough to go outside, there will be no stopping them.

WOLF BITES

Wolf greetings.

Wolves greet each other enthusiastically. They wag their tails like domestic dogs and lick each other's faces. They jump up and run around and roll over and nip at each other. That's not surprising when you consider that some wolves may have been away from the pack for days hunting. Lesser wolves will also stick their noses in their leader's face, which is a wolf's way of saying, "You're stronger than I am; please be nice to me." Sometimes they all begin howling together—even the pups—which is a little like the wolf equivalent of a human family sing-along.

LEFT: **Wolf pups like this black one are naturally curious and often start investigating their rainforest home at a very young age.**

RIGHT: **This is the entrance of a typical wolf den, dug under an old western red cedar tree. Some den sites are used year after year and are connected to other nearby dens by underground tunnels.**

TOP: **Most of the Great Bear Rainforest isn't actually a forest like this one. It's made up of rocks, ice fields, bogs and glaciers. But it's in the forest where most of the animals live, and where you'll find its towering trees, including hemlocks, spruces and cedars.**

They'll be like kids with a toy when they sniff the outdoors for the first time and take their first tentative steps into the rainforest. And when they do, it will mean spring is well on its way.

In the rainforest, April means spring has finally arrived. Near the coast, all the snow that fell during the winter has disappeared. There's still some higher up, in the mountains, but at sea level the ground is getting greener all the time. Everywhere you look, new shoots are pushing through the rich rainforest soil as plants of every kind reach toward the rays of sunlight that filter through the trees. The sun is still pretty low in the sky, so it's not very strong. But it's getting stronger all the time, and that's all the rainforest's plants need to grow.

One of the most curious things about the Great Bear Rainforest is that most of it isn't a forest at all. More than two-thirds is made up of mountains, glaciers, ice fields and bogs. But it's in the forests where most animals, including wolves, live, and where you'll find its giant evergreens—the towering hemlocks, spruces and cedars. Much of the Great Bear Rainforest is still old-growth forest, meaning it's never been logged, burned or otherwise destroyed. Consequently, the evergreen trees in the forest have been around a very long time—more than a thousand years in some cases. That's old enough to have been growing long before Christopher Columbus landed in North America. And when you have that much time to grow, you grow awfully big. The biggest rainforest trees can be almost one hundred meters tall—as tall as the world-famous Big Ben clock tower in London.

Spring is always welcome in the rainforest. After the long cold winter, the increasing light and warmth that spring brings enable the giant evergreens to sprout a whole new set of light green needles over their dark winter boughs, giving them a temporary two-toned appearance. For a short time it's almost as if they can't decide which color green to be.

Deciduous trees— the alders, cottonwoods, maples and willows that grow among the evergreens—go a step further. They lose their leaves entirely in the fall and then grow fresh ones in spring. After a winter snowfall they look like gray skeletons dressed in white robes. Or if they're not dressed in snow, they're probably dripping wet thanks to the sheets of rain that can fall each day. In the wettest parts of the Great Bear

WOLF BITES

Choosing a den site.

Although we can never know what really goes on in a wolf's head, one thing we have learned is that there are a lot of similarities between coastal wolf dens. Den locations are usually sheltered from the wind. They have ready access to fresh water and food, and they're usually near the center of the wolf family's territory—the most secure place there is for a wolf. This also ensures they're as far away as possible from other wolf dens. An especially interesting observation is that dens are often built near patches of thick vegetation such as salal bush. Salal, a common shrub in the Great Bear Rainforest, crackles when you walk through it. So if the den is surrounded by salal, the bushes could act as an alarm system to warn the family of an intruder's approach. Consequently, getting near a wolf den undetected is a very difficult thing to do.

Rainforest it can rain as much as five meters, or fifteen feet, a year. But in spring there can be days when it doesn't rain at all. Instead the sun will shine and the sky will turn from slate gray to a pale and pleasing shade of blue, and everywhere you look new green leaves are getting brighter and brighter.

However, it's not just the forest's plants that are renewing themselves. Just like the wolves, animals all over the Great Bear Rainforest are giving birth at this time too. The rainforest's famous bears—black bears, grizzlies and white spirit bears—are raising cubs. At sea, killer whales are having calves, and seals and sea lions are having pups. In dens buried both deep and shallow beneath the forest floor, mice are having mice, martens are having martens, and wolverines are having wolverines. And high up in the forest canopy

BOTTOM: **A flock of Canada geese lands on a rainforest river. Wolves will hunt geese, ducks and other birds but have never been known to hunt or eat ravens.**

in nests built inside tree cavities or balanced neatly on sturdy branches, eagles, ravens, woodpeckers and jays are hatching chicks.

Most important to the rainforest's wolves, however, Sitka black-tailed deer are having fawns. These tan-colored animals with white chins, white backsides and—guess what—black tails are the most important and dependable food source coastal wolves have. In fact, when wolf pups come out of their dens and start eating meat, it very likely will be the flesh of these young deer they'll bite into. When the pups' family goes hunting—eventually the pups will be expected to come along too—the youngest, tastiest deer are saved for the clan's newest members. Why? Researchers aren't sure, but it could be because, just as in human families, wolf families like to spoil their babies and give them the softest, most delicious pieces of meat.

TOP: **The Sitka black-tailed deer is a rainforest wolf's favorite prey. Wherever deer go, wolves follow. Over 70 percent of a coastal wolf's diet is made up of deer meat.**

WOLF BITES

What are some of the differences between wolves and dogs?

The main difference between wolves and dogs, of course, is that wolves are wild and dogs are domesticated or tame. But there are other differences too. Unlike dogs, wolves rarely bark. And when they do, their bark is quite different than a dog's. A wolf's bark is a sharp muffled sound. Wolves also have proportionally larger feet, longer legs and a broader skull than most dogs. And a wolf's muzzle is typically longer than a dog's. When wolves trot, their hind legs move on the same line as their forelegs. When a dog runs, it places its hind legs between its forelegs. Wolves can eat a lot more at one time than a dog. This is necessary because it may be days or even weeks before they get another meal.

RIGHT: **Ever since European settlers arrived on North American shores, they have waged war on the wolf. By contrast, First Nations people have always admired and respected wolves like this handsome fellow.**

Or the reason could be more practical. The older a deer is, the more parasites it will carry. A wolf pup's immune system—the system of proteins in the pup's body that help ward off disease—isn't as developed as it is in older wolves, so meat from an older deer may not be as safe for a wolf pup as meat from a young one.

When you think how cute and fragile young fawns are, it may be upsetting to picture them being killed by wolves. Perhaps the nineteenth-century English poet Alfred, Lord Tennyson, put it best when he wrote that nature is "red in tooth and claw." This was his way of saying how raw and bloody nature can be. But bloody or not, this is how it works. In nature, everything feeds off everything else. So wolves, being strict meat eaters, have no choice but to hunt and kill deer and other animals for food. They can't survive any other way. And don't forget that if they weren't there to keep the number of deer down, there would be so many deer that they'd destroy the forest by eating every plant and shrub in sight. This would mean instead of dying quickly in a wolf's jaws, some deer would starve slowly and painfully, and the forest would no longer be what nature intended it to be.

This is precisely what happened on a chain of islands called Haida Gwaii, just shy of a hundred kilometers (sixty-two miles) west of the Great Bear Rainforest. As far as scientists can tell, deer, wolves, grizzly bears and cougars were never meant to inhabit these islands. But early European settlers decided, as they so often did, to flout nature's rules and introduce deer to the islands anyway. So they shipped some over from the mainland. And when they did, they learned

WOLF BITES

Family hierarchy.

At the top of the family or pack are the alpha male and female. They stand upright, hold their heads, ears and tails erect, and look other wolves directly in the eye. They're the king and queen of their pack. Below them are a middle class of non-breeding adults and perhaps an underclass of adults who live on the fringe of the pack. In the presence of higher-ranking members of the pack, they cower, keep their tails low and their ears pulled back. They may even lie on their backs and expose their soft underbellies, the most vulnerable part of any animal. There also may be up-and-comers in the family. These young wolves, usually younger than two years of age, have yet to decide their futures. Will they stay with the family and continue to pay homage to the alpha male and female, or will they strike out on their own and find a new place in the rainforest? Or maybe they'll bide their time in hopes of taking over the pack one day.

an important lesson. With no predators to control the population, it exploded. There are now so many deer on Haida Gwaii that they're destroying the forest. Each young cedar tree that emerges is quickly eaten, so in large parts of the islands there are no new generations of cedar trees to replace the old ones. When you walk through the rainforest, it is devoid of understory (the name scientists give the shrubs and plants growing under the main forest canopy). Instead it's open and barren—completely different from the lush multi-layered rainforest across Hecate Strait where wolves and deer live in balance.

The way everything connects with everything else in nature is what makes the rainforest so complex and productive. The wolves eat the deer who eat the leaves that grow on the trees and bushes that are fed by the nutrients in the soil. And what helps feed the soil? The forest's animals. When they die or drop their feces, tiny organisms break them down so that, over time, what was once a whole wolf or whale or salmon is reduced to nothing but microscopic organisms. This is the never-ending cycle of life. Nothing lasts forever except this cycle. The rainforest's plants are no different. When they wilt and die, they feed the rainforest too. Have you ever heard the expression "the sum of its parts"? Well, we're all the sum of our parts. The rainforest is too. And some of its parts can be very small indeed.

Families are made up of parts too. Think of yours. As well as your parents, you may have brothers and sisters, grandparents, cousins, and aunts and uncles. They're all part of you, and you're part of them.

A coastal wolf family is the same. Unlike a rainforest bear, who will live most of his or her life alone, wolves live in family groups. Sometimes that family can be as small as two wolves—usually two young wolves who have struck out on their own and haven't had pups yet. Think of a young married couple leaving town for a new life somewhere else. Wolves are the same. As many as 20 percent of all rainforest wolves are known as *extra-territorials* or *dispersers*. These are wolves who wander the rainforest in search of a new pack to join or a vacant territory where they can begin a new pack of their own. You've probably heard the expression "a lone wolf," meaning a person who goes his or her own way. It comes from these wandering wolves. But by and large lone wolves are the exceptions. Most wolves

TOP: **While it may look to a casual observer as if wolves just play all day, they are actually forming a very important social structure within their pack. The dynamics of the pack are always changing, and one day, based on the outcome of play like this, one of these wolves may take over as leader.**

WOLF BITES

How long does a wolf live?

Lifespan depends on how easy or difficult that animal's life is. If there's lots of food around and the wolf isn't injured during a hunt, or by other wolves or a human, he or she might live ten or more years. In zoos, gray wolves, which are the coastal wolves' larger cousins, have been known to live as long as thirteen years. Like domestic dogs, wolves grow very fast. They reach their full size in just one year, but they're typically not ready to start mating and having pups of their own until they're two.

RIGHT: **Because they live by the sea, rainforest wolves eat more than just land animals. At low tide they can forage for barnacles, mussels and crabs. With luck, they may even come across a beached seal or sea lion.**

are social animals that need to live in packs or families to survive.

Sometimes a wolf family can contain as many as fifteen members, each one playing an important role in keeping the family together. Leading the family are the alpha male and female. The alpha male, usually the biggest, strongest wolf, will decide when to hunt and what to hunt for. He also keeps his family together by keeping all the other wolves in line. And he will usually father all the family's pups. The alpha female is his mate. She takes charge of defending the family and choosing where to build a birthing den.

Occasionally, if the food supply is especially generous, another member of the wolf family may breed too, and the pack will have more than one set of pups. But this is very rare among rainforest wolves.

In between the alpha male and female and their newborn pups are approximately five to ten other wolves who help bring up the young, hunt and kill prey and protect the wolf family's territory from intruders like bears, cougars and other wolves. Each family member will fulfill his or her own special duty according to his or her own personality and place. If you've ever seen puppies in a litter, you'll know it doesn't take long for each pup to develop his or her own personality. One will be bold; another shy. One curious; another nervous. Wolf pups are the same. Right from the time they're born, their games help establish a kind of brother-and-sister pecking order with one pup—usually the strongest, bravest one— on top and the rest following behind. When you

think about it, human families aren't very different. Every child has his or her own personality, and that personality often determines what he or she will do later in life. And we all know that in every school-yard there are kids who lead and kids who follow.

Later, as the pups grow older, and if a hunter or disease hasn't killed them, they may choose to leave the family to strike out on their own and establish their own families and territories. Some may be forced out if the pack has become too large for the amount of food available to it. Usually the wolves who leave are the bolder, more independent animals who don't want to live the rest of their lives under the paws of their mothers and fathers. Other pups are content to play a more subservient role. They don't mind leaving the big decisions to other members of the family. They prefer to do what they're told rather than tell others what to do. Again, just like people.

And just think: this all starts from the moment they leave the den and see the magnificent rainforest for the first time.

WOLF BITES

How do coastal wolves differ from inland gray wolves?

Coastal wolves are about 20 percent smaller and lighter than their gray cousins. A good many of them have reddish or ocher-colored fur, while gray wolves are—guess what—mainly gray or silver. The coastal wolf's fur is also less dense because the air temperature is warmer along the coast than it is in the BC interior. At least it is in winter. And they rely on seafood—fish, seals, crustaceans, etc.—for a large portion of their diet.

LEFT: **The oceanside environment is a beautiful place of different colors and textures, but the rainforest wolves who live in it have to remain alert for both prey and predators.**

RIGHT: **The Great Bear Rainforest** is a breathtaking jigsaw puzzle of landmasses and waterways. Everywhere you turn along the coast there is another island, bay, fjord or inlet. Inland there are countless lakes, rivers and streams. Because water is such an integral part of the rainforest, rainforest wolves have evolved to make use of it. They swim from island to island in search of prey. They comb seashores for crabs, barnacles and mussels, and in the fall they fish for salmon. That's why some scientists refer to BC's coastal wolves as marine mammals.

CHAPTER THREE

Summertime and the Livin' Is Easier

Ask anyone what his or her favorite time of year is—especially any kid who's off school—and the answer probably will be summer. And why not? The weather is warm and sunny, and it doesn't rain much. And almost everything is in season. When else do you get fresh raspberries, blueberries, cherries and peaches? Summer is also when the grass in your lawn grows tallest and thickest, and when the trees in your backyard are heaviest with leaves.

In the Great Bear Rainforest the weather is also at its best during the summer. The rain still falls, but not as much. The wind still blows, but not as hard. The sky can still be gray and cloudy, but it turns blue more often. And in the middle of June, when the sun is at its highest point, it hardly gets dark at all. You can go outside and read a book at ten o'clock in the evening or four in the morning.

LEFT: **Unlike domestic dogs, who will imitate their sleepy human companions, wild wolves don't yawn because they're tired, but because they're anxious.**

Summer is also when almost every kind of plant in the rainforest is at its best. Wild berries become ripe and juicy. Ferns and horsetails that vanished into the earth over winter reach for the sky again. Sedge, a grasslike plant that looks like a long green saber, grows as high as a grizzly bear's eye. In fact, the rainforest floor all but disappears under an explosion of new plants struggling for a place in the now warm sun.

For animals living in the rainforest, summer, like spring, is also a welcome change. Many animals—bears, marmots, bats, frogs, newts and snakes among them—spend winter asleep underground. Insect eggs laid in the fall lie dormant until spring. Most birds have flown south. But in summer, when the temperature rises and the plants come back to life, animals

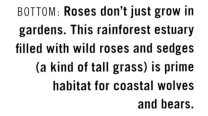

BOTTOM: **Roses don't just grow in gardens. This rainforest estuary filled with wild roses and sedges (a kind of tall grass) is prime habitat for coastal wolves and bears.**

come to life too. Many birds have returned north and now perch in trees. Beavers build dams. Tadpoles swim. Fawns explore. Sandhill cranes roost with their newborn chicks. Humpback and killer whales breach, dive and slap their tails. Bees pollinate flowers, and the bears of the Great Bear Rainforest stuff their faces with berries.

For wolves and deer, summer is welcome too, though for different reasons. Unlike bears, who sleep the winter away, wolves and deer are active all year. This means they never stop searching for food, and in December and January that can be tough. So tough that some wolves and deer don't make it to spring. But in summer the living is easy—or at least easier. Food is everywhere. The rainforest is a banquet—a green feast nature has laid out for her many residents.

TOP: **Old-growth temperate rainforest is among the rarest forest type on Earth. One of the many reasons the Great Bear Rainforest is so special is that it contains a quarter of all the temperate rainforest left in the world.**

WOLF BITES

How well do wolves smell?

Very well. Wolves are said to be able to smell a moose 2 kilometers (1.2 miles) away. That's why the scent marks they leave for other wolves are so important. Just from sniffing one of these scent marks, a wolf is said to be able to tell which sex of wolf was last there, who was traveling with whom, and how long it's been since the area was hunted.

RIGHT: **Wolves are usually born in dens hidden deep in the rainforest, but when the cubs are old enough to travel short distances, the pack will often move to what's called a rendezvous site. These sites are usually close to the ocean, where wolf pups can forage for food when the tide goes out.**

In winter, wolves, who eat only meat, have to rely on deer (their main staple), moose, river otter and mountain goats to fill their stomachs because so many of the smaller animals they hunt—marmots, beavers, voles and mice among them—are underground or in dens, And hunting larger animals can be dangerous. A buck or bull moose has a tremendously powerful back kick, and a wolf who finds him- or herself on the receiving end of one can be crippled for life. In summer, with many more different kinds of prey available, hunting isn't as treacherous. Small animals obviously don't provide the same kind of meal a deer or moose does, but there are lots of them around.

Regardless of the time of year, the most important question that hangs over every hunt is whether the wolves will gain more energy from hunting than they'll lose. What does this mean, exactly? Put it this way: suppose you had to walk ten kilometers every day to get a peanut-butter sandwich. At the same time, suppose your body needed two peanut-butter sandwiches a day to survive. That would mean you'd have to walk twenty kilometers every day to get your two sandwiches. But that's a lot of walking, and you'd expend a lot of energy doing it. So before you started, you might ask yourself: Is it worth it? Should you risk expending all the energy it takes to walk twenty kilometers for the promise of two peanut-butter sandwiches? What if, when you finished the twenty kilometers, the sandwiches were no longer there? What then? Wolves face this kind of dilemma all the time. When they plan a hunt, they can't be

WOLF BITES

How big is a wolf family territory?

That depends on the amount of prey the territory can support. If prey is abundant, a territory can be as small as 60 square kilometers (37 square miles) for a family of as many as ten animals. This abundance of prey is why rainforest wolves have some of the smallest home-range territories of any wolf populations in the world. The alpha male and female wolves mark their territories' borders by peeing on stumps, logs, growing trees and rocks. That way, if a wolf from another family sniffs the pee, he or she will know to go no farther. In wolf language these markers are like No Trespassing signs. In fact, scientists know of instances when a pack of wolves has stopped chasing a deer or moose when its prey had the good fortune to cross into another wolf family's territory. Deer also have learned to spend more time on the edges of wolf territories because they know wolf packs try to avoid direct contact with non-family members. So deer go where wolves are afraid to.

sure they won't burn more energy going after a deer or moose than they'll gain in bringing their prey down. Remember, not every hunt is successful. Deer and moose get away all the time. So it's a hard decision—especially for an animal that doesn't have a refrigerator to store food for long periods of time.

This is also why a wolf will sometimes let a healthy deer walk by without a chase. Wolves have to weigh this balance every time they consider hunting. In summer, when there's more food around, these decisions are easier to make. But even summer brings wolves special pressures in the form of caring for pups. Usually an adult is deputized to look after the young. But what if, for some reason, this adult is needed on a hunt too? What should the wolf family do? Leave the pups on their own and expose them to possible harm? Or leave the adult behind and risk the hunt's success? Who knows? Sometimes when pups are too young to take part in a hunt and too young to travel, adults may choose to hunt near the den. But this can limit the amount of prey available to them. Or they may decide to move the pups farther away to what's known as a rendezvous site. These sites, which are considered safe zones for pups, are scattered throughout the rainforest, usually within a kilometer or so of the den door. If the wolves can do this, their food supply may be that much greater. But again, they don't know for sure. You can see how decisions are a big part of a coastal wolf's day.

However, wolves do their best hunting at night. Their eyes are built specially to see in the dark, and their excellent sense of smell allows them to track

prey in all kinds of weather. They also work coop-
eratively. A single wolf can be a good hunter, but
nothing like a family of wolves. A family will spread
out through the forest and travel silently until one of
them smells prey. If it's a deer, the wolves may circle
the animal before moving in. Sometimes the deer will
try to run for the ocean because usually it can swim
faster than a wolf. Sometimes it's so frightened it will
just run—in no particular direction. Sometimes it
sits quietly, almost as if it knows that its contribu-
tion to the rainforest, the wolves and the endless life
cycle is to give up its life. Regardless, wolves are fed
by their feet, so they will always do their utmost to
find prey and kill it. And when they do, they eat as
much as they can because when they get back to their

TOP: **Wolves are built for running,
and while they can sprint over short
distances, they are best traveling
long distances at a lope or trot.**

dens they will regurgitate, or throw up, some of it for their pups. Sometimes they will take back a whole deer leg. This gives the pups a chance to chew bones and marrow. A fresh deer kill can keep a wolf family fed for a couple of days.

Because the Great Bear Rainforest is as much about the sea as the land, it shouldn't be surprising to learn that wolves find food in its inlets, bays and fjords too. During the late summer and fall, salmon return in the millions to swim upriver and lay eggs, and when this happens, wolves feast hungrily on the fish. But wolves don't have to wait until then for the sea to serve dinner. In spring and summer as well as fall, the jagged rainforest shoreline is full of barnacles, mussels, crabs and clams for wolves to eat. That may seem strange—

to think of a wolf eating seafood. But rainforest wolves, like every other creature on the planet, adapt to where they live, and in a place defined by the sea as much as the Great Bear Rainforest is, seafood is a constant. Seafood is not the biggest part of a wolf's diet, but when you're as hungry as a wolf, every morsel helps.

Wolves also chase and eat shorebirds living along the rainforest's coasts: ducks, geese, herons and cranes. And now researchers have found that the wolves even hunt seals when they climb on land to sleep on little rocky islets called *haulouts*. A fat, blubbery seal is a big bonus for a wolf family—like having Thanksgiving turkey in the middle of summer. And if a giant squid somehow ends up on a beach, wolves won't say no to it either. While wolves normally catch and kill what they eat, they're not so fussy that they'll turn up their noses at something that's already dead, providing it hasn't been dead too long.

The part of the rainforest where the seashore slips into the ocean—what's known as the intertidal zone—is also a good place for wolves to catch land animals because it's a place that attracts river otters, mink, deer and bears. Yes, bears. Rainforest wolves hunt them occasionally. Most animals, including bears, can outswim a wolf if they get enough of a head start. But the wolf is seldom one to give up. So even while that deer or moose is swimming away, the wolf may take one last all-or-nothing leap into the water after whatever it's chasing in an attempt to land on top of it. Sometimes it works; sometimes it doesn't. On hard ground a deer or moose can use its hind legs

WOLF BITES

Do other animals prey on wolves?
Adult wolves don't have natural predators, but cougars, eagles and grizzly bears may kill and eat wolf pups if they get the chance. Humans don't eat wolves, but we do hunt and kill them for sport or their fur. Coastal wolves are not protected from hunting and trapping in BC, so they're killed all the time.

to kick a wolf. But in the water it can be a sitting—or swimming—duck.

What we know about wolves is largely the result of what First Nations people have been able to learn from watching coastal wolves firsthand for generations. As well, many recent observations have been made by scientists and conservationists. Even so, few people ever get to see a wild wolf because they're so elusive. They're also mainly nocturnal, which makes sighting one even more difficult. So if you are determined to see one, your best chance will come early in the morning or late in the day, as the sun rises or sets.

As challenging as it is to see a coastal wolf, it's worth it. Watching a rainforest family of wolves up close as they dig for clams by the seashore or tear into a whale carcass that's drifted in on the tide is a rare, remarkable and wondrous thing. It's an experience you're guaranteed never to forget.

WOLF BITES

How does a rainforest wolf differ from a German shepherd, the dog most people compare wolves to?

Even though they're both about the same size and look somewhat similar, with upright ears and a long snout, the wolf has yellow instead of brown eyes; a bigger, more powerful chest; and a straighter back. It's also a different color. While German shepherds are mainly brown and black, most rainforest wolves have a touch of red in their coat. But the main difference is that the German shepherd, no matter its temper and disposition, is a domesticated animal. A wolf is not. A wolf is wild.

LEFT: **If you see a rainforest wolf on his own, he may have left the pack he was born into to join a new pack or start one of his own. These wolves are called dispersers and are quite common.**

RIGHT: **Rainforest wolves blend into their coastal environment very well. This natural camouflage helps them disguise themselves when they're hunting.**

CHAPTER FOUR

By the Beautiful Sea

At first glance, the churning waters off the coast of the Great Bear Rainforest may seem like the last place on Earth to find a wolf. There's no open tundra or windswept prairie where herds of ungulates (what scientists call hoofed animals like deer or moose) amass like armies. But by now you've come to realize what a special place the Great Bear Rainforest is. And as it happens, the wolves of the GBR are special wolves as well. Coastal wolves are different from other wolves in a number of respects. We've already mentioned that they're smaller than their cousins on the other side of the Coast Mountains, and that their coloring is different—red/brown instead of silver/gray. Another key difference is that coastal wolves are excellent swimmers, though not the way seals are. They don't turn corkscrews and somersaults

LEFT: **Colorful sea urchins and sea stars adorn a rocky island in the heart of the Great Bear Rainforest. The forest is a place where the land and sea don't just meet; they merge.**

in the heaving surf. But they do swim—and they do it with ease and confidence.

So if you're in a canoe or a sailboat, plying your way between the hundreds of islands that litter the rainforest coastline like confetti, and you happen to cast your eye sideways or glance across the bow, there's no telling when a wolf might come dog- or wolf-paddling by. All you'll be able to see will be his or her head, held erect and safely out of the water, and the upper back sloping gently out of sight. But under the surface will be four busy paws steadily moving the wolf forward, slowly and purposefully, from one island to another. Even four-month-old pups sometimes swim with their parents. If you're not expecting it, the sight will certainly make you look twice. Even three times. Can that really be

BOTTOM: **Hundreds of islands hug the coast of the BC rainforest, and many are decorated with seaweed-soaked reefs like this one. Consequently, coastal wolves, unlike their inland cousins, make their living by hunting both land and sea creatures.**

a wolf swimming? Yes. In the Great Bear Rainforest they do it all the time.

But if you think about what kind of a place the Great Bear Rainforest is, the fact that wolves are competent swimmers only makes sense. Animals evolve according to their surroundings. Over time, as one generation gives way to another, the individuals most likely to survive and reproduce are those who can do things easily and efficiently. If the BC coastal wolf lived in a place where there was no water, knowing how to swim wouldn't matter. But in the Great Bear Rainforest the land and water don't just meet; they merge. Waves rush in from the Pacific and pound the rocks and sand. Mountain streams flow into rivers that flush into the sea. Fish return from the sea to swim up these rivers and feed the land. And trees that grow at the water's edge dig ever deeper into the earth,

TOP: **Wolves aren't equipped with the same long fishhook claws that bears have, so they have to use their jaws and teeth to catch salmon. This wolf is doing his best, but it's tough fishing in deep choppy water.**

WOLF BITES

How do wolves communicate with each other?

In all sorts of ways. In addition to the sounds that come from their mouths—howls, barks and whines—they also communicate using their sense of smell and in how they play, touch and groom one another. But perhaps most interesting is how they communicate without appearing to do or say anything at all. There are times when, without so much as a grunt or a turn of his head, an alpha male will let his family know it's time to get up and move on, almost as if the idea were one that everyone came up with in the same instant. Call it wolf telepathy.

RIGHT: **You've probably been told how important it is to drink water each day. Wolves are no different. Meat eaters like wolves need fresh water to aid their digestion.**

firming their grip on it. This is the rich, changing and, above all, diverse environment where coastal wolves make their homes, so it's no wonder they have to be comfortable in water as well as on land.

But even within the Great Bear Rainforest there are two distinct populations of coastal wolves. There are wolves who live on the mainland, and wolves who live on the many islands that hug the coast. And each kind of wolf leads a different life. Island wolves may live their whole lives without ever seeing a moose or a mountain goat—animals as familiar to mainland wolves as the fur on their paws. But why would they? Wolves and their families occupy carefully marked territories from which they rarely stray. So even though moose and mountain goats might live only a few kilometers away from an island wolf family's territory, if they never enter that island territory, the island wolves will never see them.

What mainland and island wolves do have in common is that they both eat deer. They eat lots of other animals too—big, small, landlubbing and sea-dwelling. But mainly they eat deer—the same Sitka black-tailed deer that travel swiftly and quietly through so much of the Great Bear Rainforest. Consequently, if deer live on a rainforest island, chances are wolves will live on that island too. As with almost everything in nature, there's a balance. A family of wolves needs a steady supply of deer to feed them. If there's a healthy population of deer, the wolves will be healthy too. Sometimes, however, while there may be deer on an island, there may not be enough to sustain a wolf family's needs. But what if there is a neighboring

island with deer on it? And what if next to that island is a third island with deer on it too? Individually, each of these islands may not have enough Sitka black-tailed deer to maintain a family of wolves over the long term. But put them together and they can support generations of them. The only catch is that to get from one island to another, wolves have to swim. So they do. Either that or they starve. Look out over the water and you might see a whole parade of them, nose to tail, making their way through the waves from one island to the next. When the water is calm, swimming is easy—perfect for paddling. When it's rough, it's harder and more dangerous. So wolves weigh their options carefully before they dive in.

When it comes to mainland wolves, the world they occupy is both constant and changing. It changes with the weather and the seasons, but it's also a place where giant trees stand still and steady. Not so the island wolf's home. It's a more varied place, where sandy beaches, open bogs, rocky headlands and tidal pools are pushed and pulled relentlessly by tides and storms. When you think about it, it's amazing that two groups of wolves can live so close to each other and yet lead such different lives. But to them their territories are like two planets, one defined mainly by the land and the other by the sea. And as we all know, the only predictable thing about the sea is its unpredictability. It's a wild, restless, rippling and sometimes overwhelming environment.

The sea can also be generous. For an island wolf growing up with the sound of surf in his ears, there is more than just deer meat in nature's larder. There are

WOLF BITES

What does a wolf's howl mean?
This depends on who utters the howl and under what circumstances. The length, pitch and volume of a wolf's howl will differ depending on what the wolf wants to say. And just as our voices are peculiar to us, a wolf's howl is peculiar to him or her. Every wolf has his or her own tone and style. Howling can reunite a pack if members get separated for some reason, or it might be used to signal one's presence to another pack. Sometimes wolves howl in celebration when the pack is united after a successful hunting trip. Whatever the case, if you are fortunate enough to hear wolves howling in a remote rainforest estuary, you'll know it's one of the most beautiful and haunting sounds on Earth.

LEFT: **Wolves can run very fast, and when they set their sights on a particular prey animal, they are determined. But hunting large prey, like deer or moose, is difficult— even dangerous—for a wolf on his own. This is why wolves usually hunt in packs.**

WOLF BITES

What's the difference between a bear trail and a wolf trail?

Simple: bears wander and so do their trails. Wolf trails are straight, narrow and purposeful because wolves always seem to know where they're going. They travel in single file and move from hunting spot to hunting spot in as straight a line as possible. And because wolves travel so often along the same paths, over time even their padded paws can wear down a piece of ground. Of course, wolves and bears often share trails too. Throughout the GBR there are old established trails, usually running alongside rivers and streams, that are used by a multitude of wildlife.

RIGHT: **The ocean can turn up all sorts of meals for a wild wolf— everything from barnacles to sea lions. Rainforest wolves don't have a hope of catching a seal or sea lion at sea, but on land it's a different story.**

also shore- and seabirds that flock to intertidal areas to gather food and fish. Birds like cranes, geese and herons also make good use of islands, building nests on them and raising their young. Any of them can make a tasty meal for a wolf.

And while a land animal like a wolf couldn't possibly hope to catch a seal at sea, it's a different story on land. Sometimes seals like to haul themselves out of the ocean to rest and sleep. And as they sleep, the tide goes out, separating them farther and farther from the water's edge. Uh-oh. This is what wolves wait for. Have you ever seen a seal move around on land? If you have, you'll know that they're not nearly as fast on land as they are in water, and that's good news for a wolf. Usually a wolf will manage to take the seal by surprise. The interesting and unfair part of all this is that one of the reasons seals rest on rocks is to avoid orcas, or killer whales, coincidentally known as "wolves of the sea." Yet another example of how "red in tooth and claw" nature can be.

Of course, with so much water around, there are fish too. Island wolves don't plunge into the waves after fish the way seals or seabirds do, but given the strong ocean currents and crashing surf that roars in from the Pacific, there's no telling when a fish, whale or seal might wash up on shore. And when it does, wolves devour it. There are also all the creatures of the intertidal zone—the crabs, clams, mussels and barnacles that live on and under the shoreline rocks and sand. Individually they're not much more than an hors d'oeuvre for an animal the size of a wolf. But when there are enough of them, they become a meal.

Not only that; small animals like these can be hunting starter kits for pups. The pups can chase them and sharpen their teeth and claws on animals they know won't fight back. There are not many places in the world that provide newly born wolves the same kind of opportunity for a successful hunt—even if the quarry is only a small crab or a barnacle.

During the spring and summer, island wolves, like their mainland cousins, also enjoy good days in the rainforest. There is less rain, the air is warmer and the wolves have shed their winter coats. Food is plentiful too. The air and land are buzzing, squawking and squealing with potential prey. So this is the time when island pups learn both how to hunt and how to engage socially within their family. Island life is also less dangerous for pups than mainland life because there are fewer predators like bears and cougars that can catch and kill wolf pups living on the islands. So when the tide goes out, pups can safely play tug-of-war with the seaweed they find on the beach or romp in the ocean foam that burbles off the waves like bubble bath.

But come early autumn, life for all rainforest wolves will change again. In fact, for a short time it will get much better. By September, rainforest wolves, whether they live on the mainland or on an island, enjoy the greatest bounty the sea has to offer—the return of millions of salmon to their rivers of birth. And when that happens, the wolves do something surprising: they go fishing.

WOLF BITES

Birds in the Great Bear Rainforest.
There are migratory birds that fly north in the summer and south in the winter, and there are resident birds that live on the coast all year long. Gulls, herons, geese and bald eagles are some of the year-round residents, while sandpipers, ospreys, sandhill cranes and hummingbirds visit the rainforest to nest and raise their young in the summer before heading south again.

LEFT: **When the tide goes out, the seashore reveals its bounty. This family of wolves is resting just below the tide line, where, if they're hungry, they're bound to find all sorts of tasty snacks.**

65

RIGHT: **Forests are made up of more than just trees. At sea they're made up of kelp. In fact, kelp forests are among the most beautiful and biologically productive environments on earth. They are found throughout the world in shallow, cool, open coastal waters, including those along the Great Bear Rainforest. At the surface of Pacific kelp forests like this one, the kelp often have long stems called stipes. One end of the stem is anchored to rocks on the sea floor, and the other boasts a gasbag that keeps the kelp afloat.**

CHAPTER FIVE

The Salmon Wolves

If it's hard to imagine a wolf swimming or hunting seals, how about one fishing for salmon? In the Great Bear Rainforest they do it every fall. Between August and November, salmon that have spent two to four years swimming in the Pacific Ocean reappear in the millions to fight their way up the rainforest's rivers and streams to spawn and die. Many don't make it. Instead they become food for killer whales, seals, sea lions, bears, eagles, people or wolves. Coastal wolves could easily be called fishing wolves because of their fondness for salmon.

In fact, wolves like the taste of salmon almost as much as bears do. Except, when it comes to catching the fish, wolves are at a bit of a disadvantage because they don't have the long, curved, fishing-hook claws of a bear. Instead they have to use their mouths.

LEFT: **Because of their fondness for salmon, coastal wolves are sometimes known as fishing wolves. This wet wolf going after a salmon on a bright fall morning illustrates why. A pack of wolves can catch more than two hundred salmon in a single evening of fishing.**

WOLF BITES

Do wolves fish alone?

Yes. When hunting larger animals like deer or moose, wolves mainly operate as packs or families, but when it comes to catching a salmon, a group effort isn't necessary. However, if salmon runs are especially rich, wolves and bears will sometimes put aside their traditional enmity and fish alongside one another. Wolves have even been observed fishing in deep water by going right under— just like a seal—in search of salmon.

RIGHT: **This coastal wolf is about to enjoy a meal of chum salmon after a successful fishing expedition. Given the choice, some coastal wolves would rather hunt salmon than deer. It's not hard to understand why. Deer kick. Salmon don't.**

Even so, they're very efficient. In a single night, one pack of wolves can catch more than two hundred salmon. But as with most good parties, the end result can be a mess. After a big night's fishing, salmon bodies litter the riverbank like leaves after a wind. And if you think those bodies don't stink, think again. If you smelled them, you'd wish you had a clothes-peg on your nose. But once you get over the stink and look closer, you'll notice that none of the bodies has a head. It's as if they've been guillotined. Why? Because the head is the only part of the salmon wolves like to eat.

Why wolves eat the salmon's head is a mystery. One theory is that there are parasites in the rest of the salmon's body that are harmful to wolves, so they've learned over time to eat only the heads. Another theory is that wolves simply prefer the fattier heads. Just as many humans will eat only certain parts of an animal, so will wolves. Or it could be due to something else entirely. At this point scientists simply don't know. But while we don't know why they eat the salmon heads, we do know that all those headless salmon bodies have a big impact on the rainforest. When the wolves move on and leave them lying there, stinking to high heaven, all kinds of scavengers get busy breaking them down. Birds peck at the skin and flesh. Insects invade the guts and eat them from the inside out. Then different kinds of bacteria get busy breaking apart every last bit of them, so when all is said and done, you won't see a shred of salmon skin or flesh anywhere on the ground. Perhaps there will be a few white fish bones hidden in the moss, but that's all. However, that doesn't mean the salmon

have disappeared. Far from it. They've merely been broken down into tinier and tinier pieces so that even the plants in the rainforest—including the giant evergreens that grow nearly a hundred meters high—can take them up in their roots and be enriched by them. Any gardener will tell you that fish fertilizer is good for a garden. If the trees of the Great Bear Rainforest could talk, they'd say the same thing.

So important is the salmon to the rainforest that it's no exaggeration to say almost everything in the forest owes its survival in some way to these big silver fish. This is why some people call the GBR the Salmon Forest. Even animals who don't feed directly on them—animals such as deer, moose and Canada geese—eat plants that have been fertilized by them. This is why salmon are known as a "keystone" species,

BOTTOM: **When a family of wolves has finished fishing a river, its banks will be littered with headless salmon. Wolves prefer the heads and brains of salmon because they are the fattiest and richest parts of the fish.**

meaning they're like the main stone in an arch. Have you ever seen an old medieval or Roman arch in which each rock helps support the others? Well, imagine the rainforest salmon—the pink, Chinook, coho, sockeye and chum salmon—as one of those stones. If you pull it out, the entire arch will collapse. Same with the salmon. If you pull them out of the rainforest, the rainforest will collapse.

Salmon are so familiar to us in sandwiches and on barbecues that it's easy to take them for granted. But we shouldn't. They are one of the most remarkable species on Earth. If you disagree, take a moment to consider how they live. In the spring, millions upon millions of them hatch from eggs laid and fertilized the previous fall. They're tiny when they're born—smaller than your smallest finger. But they grow—fast. Some, like coho, spend up to three years

TOP: **Runs of sockeye salmon have become rare on the coast, so wolves only get a chance to catch them in certain rivers. But when they do, they are happy to feast on their rich and fatty flesh. All sorts of rainforest animals depend on salmon for a good part of their nourishment, but because of overfishing, pollution, climate change and disease caused by commercial salmon farms, the future of wild salmon in the Pacific is anything but certain.**

WOLF BITES

Fish farms.

Fish farms are a lot like regular farms on land. The big difference is that instead of raising pigs and cows in a pen on grass or dirt, these farms raise salmon in ocean pens. This may seem like a smart idea, but we now know such farms cause wild salmon terrible problems. One is that fish farmers raise Atlantic salmon, which don't belong in the Pacific Ocean. So when pens are damaged in a storm and fish escape, they can spread parasites and disease to native Pacific salmon and compete for food and spawning grounds. As well, fish farms are breeding grounds for sea lice, tiny parasitic creatures that feed on, and kill, young salmon. Sea lice exist in nature, but they proliferate in such great numbers in fish farms that they can do terrible damage to wild populations.

in the river or stream where they were born, getting ready to head out to sea; others, like chum and pink, migrate to sea soon after they hatch. But eventually, if they aren't eaten first, all rainforest salmon make their way down to the mouths of the rivers that empty into the Pacific and begin a life of mystery. Yes, mystery in the sense that for however long salmon live in the ocean—two to five years, depending on the species—we don't know exactly where they go or what they do. We know they swim thousands of kilometers and do their best to avoid predators. But we know very little about where they swim, how much they eat and under what circumstances. We also don't know why they live in the ocean as long as they do. Why does one species (the pink) spend two years in the ocean, and the others (the sockeye, coho, chum and Chinook) four years? And perhaps most amazing of all, how, after all that time at sea, do they know how to get back to the same river they were born in, and sometimes even the exact same spot within that river? Some scientists think they do it with a kind of built-in compass that works in concert with an ability to identify the unique smell of a particular river. No matter the exact explanation, it's fantastic. Amazing. Beyond the measure of our most powerful computers. But then so much of nature is.

The fact that wolves on the BC coast fish for salmon is also something scientists haven't known very long. They've known for years that killer whales, seals and sea lions eat salmon. And the sight of a big black or grizzly bear dipping its paw into a river and bringing out a silver salmon is something familiar

to most of us thanks to books, TV and the Internet. But fishing wolves? Until this century they weren't something people outside the Great Bear Rainforest knew much about. But to First Nations people who have lived in the temperate rainforest as long as the wolves, they're as familiar as sea stars. After all, they've watched, studied and revered the coastal wolf for generations. However, to outsiders—people who have begun to investigate the Great Bear Rainforest only in the last couple of decades—it's a wonder. Something to open your eyes wide at when you see it for the first time.

Wolves fish with their mouths, their wits and their cunning. When they see a salmon approach, they step gingerly into the water and face upriver.

TOP: **Coastal wolves have developed different fishing tricks over time. One is to always stay behind the fish.**

LEFT: **This pup is taking the easy way when it comes to fishing. The salmon he's going after is already dead, and its head is already eaten. It probably was caught and discarded upriver by a fellow pack member.**

That is, in the same direction the fish are swimming. Why? Maybe it's because they're clever enough to know that if they stand behind the fish, the fish won't see them. Then they plant their paws firmly on the streambed and, in a finger snap, plunge their muzzles into the water. The next thing you know, they've got a big silver salmon flapping in their jaws. But wolves don't eat the salmon then and there. First they take it to the side of the river and drop it on the ground. Then they place both front paws on it to stop it from squirming, and only then do they bite into its head. When they're finished, they leave what's left of the salmon lying where they dropped it, lick their lips and either return to fishing or leave to do something else.

Coastal wolves may not fish with the flair of rainforest bears, who employ all kinds of nifty moves when they go fishing in the fall. But researchers who study wolves say they usually catch one of every three fish they chase, which isn't a bad average. They also eat a lot more salmon than expected. It turns out that even if there are a lot of Sitka black-tailed deer around, wolves still choose to fish. And why not? If you were a wolf, what would you rather chase? A deer with sharp, dangerous hooves that could kick you in the face? Or a salmon, a creature with no defenses to speak of, that practically slides into your waiting jaws? True, if you killed a deer there would be a lot more meat to eat. But when you consider how many salmon swim up rainforest streams each fall and how good wolves are at catching them, they sound more and more like the sensible alternative. And nature is nothing if not sensible.

What isn't surprising is that island wolves depend more on salmon than their mainland cousins. In fact, during the fall, island wolves get most of their food from the ocean, and most of that food is salmon. Some mainland wolves rely on salmon for about half their diet. Even so, it's a lot, and it shows how important salmon are to coastal wolves, no matter where they live. But even though coastal wolves probably have been fishing for as long as there have been wolves and salmon, there's no guarantee the fish will always be there. The ancient relationship between wolves and salmon is now being tested as never before. In recent years, some of the rivers in the Great Bear Rainforest have turned *silent*—a term meaning empty of fish.

WOLF BITES

Salmon in the northwest Pacific.

There are five species of salmon—sockeye, pink, chum, Chinook and coho—as well as two species of trout—cutthroat and steelhead. Each is different from the others in terms of how long they live in fresh and salt water, how big they grow, and how many years they live. But they are all anadromous, meaning they migrate between fresh and salt water. And all of them face a tremendously difficult journey when they leave the ocean and swim back upstream to spawn. In fact, only a few make it to the end. When they do, female salmon lay their eggs in a gravel streambed, and males fertilize them. Their mission complete, they die.

And when there are no fish in a river, there are no seagulls, ravens, eagles, bears, otters or wolves there either. Hence the silence.

Why the fish disappear is still a mystery, but it's a safe bet to assume humankind is to blame. Overfishing, the harmful effects of fish farms and the destruction of the salmon's spawning grounds have all contributed to the steady and alarming disappearance of salmon up and down the BC coast. More recently, scientists have added climate change to the list of potential causes of declining salmon populations because they've learned that even a subtle change in ocean temperature makes it difficult for these fish to survive. In other words, the only certain thing about the future of salmon and the wolves who eat them is that it's more uncertain than ever.

Nature often takes thousands of years to establish her rhythms and cycles, and animals don't evolve new behaviors overnight. So if the salmon, a food source that coastal wolves have depended on for generations, disappears from the Great Bear Rainforest, there's no telling what the wolves will do. We already know what happens to rainforest bears who don't get enough fish to eat. If they don't die themselves, they're not healthy enough to have cubs. And a population of bears too sick to reproduce is a population on the brink of extinction. It's likely that the same could be said of rainforest wolves.

WOLF BITES

What other rainforest creatures benefit from salmon?

More than 190 species benefit from the rainforest's annual salmon runs, including killer whales, sharks, sea lions, seals, otters, bears, loons, mergansers (a kind of duck), herons, kingfishers, various aquatic and terrestrial insects, algae, mosses, terrestrial herbs, shrubs and trees. Rainforest mink time the birth of their pups so that they nurse these pups during the annual salmon run.

LEFT: **Even though wolves only eat salmon heads, none of the fish is wasted. When the wolves have had their fill, rainforest scavengers get busy breaking down the rest of the fish into tinier and tinier pieces so that even the rainforest soil benefits from it. This natural fish fertilizer is one of the reasons the forest is so productive.**

RIGHT: **First Nations people have always known about coastal wolves' prowess as fishermen. But it came as a surprise to scientists who began studying these animals toward the end of the last century. Now they know that during the fall, island wolves rely on salmon for most of their food, while mainland wolves rely on the fish for about half their diet. In other words, if coastal salmon were to disappear, there's every reason to fear that coastal wolves would vanish too.**

CHAPTER SIX

Winter Wandering

Winter is a time when many rainforest plants and animals disappear or hide. Although the enormous evergreen trees remain green no matter what the weather throws at them, the deciduous trees—the alders, maples and cottonwoods—lose their leaves so that only their trunks and branches silhouette against the sky. Many smaller plants, like ferns, cow parsnip and angelica, disintegrate to their roots. Berry bushes lose their leaves, and the few berries that do remain shrivel to fragile ornaments to be scavenged by birds that haven't flown south.

Most of the birds that crisscrossed the rainforest's skies and chattered in its branches during the spring and summer have left. The insects that buzzed and flitted over its ponds and marshes have laid eggs that now lie dormant in the ground. Mating and laying

LEFT: **Wolf pups are no different than human children when it comes to wanting and needing their parents. These pups are wondering where the adults in their family have gone. Most likely they've gone hunting, and if the hunt is successful, the adults will bring back the tastiest parts of the kill for the pups.**

WOLF BITES

What's a clear-cut?

As its name suggests, a clear-cut is an area of forest where every last tree has been cut down. For a long time this was the most common way for logging companies to get their timber because it is cheaper and easier. And for many years humans did not value the rainforest for anything except making two-by-fours or paper. Today some logging is done in a more selective way. Only certain trees are harvested and the rest are left alone. But clear-cutting is still common. When a forest is clear-cut, initially smaller plants such as bushes grow in the place of trees, and for a while these bushes can provide food for deer and bears. And if there are more deer around, that's good news for rainforest wolves. But only in the short run. Food in a clear-cut isn't as nutritious as food in a rainforest that's been left alone, and clear-cuts don't protect the deer from the deep snow. So in the long run the deer will suffer, which means wolves will suffer too.

RIGHT: **Every member of a wolf family knows and understands his or her role in it. That's why wolf families work so efficiently.**

eggs is one of the last things adult insects do. When they finish, they die. Rough-skinned newts that swam along the surface of ponds when the sky was blue have buried themselves in mud now that it's gray. And snakes that used to slither along the sun-soaked rainforest floor now huddle under rocks in a semi-comatose state.

The salmon that filled the forest's rivers and streams in the fall have all spawned and died. The carcasses left behind by wolves and bears have been picked clean by scavengers. All that's left of them are a few bones lying at the bottom of the creeks and rivers. The eggs female salmon laid and males fertilized lie like little beads in gravel beds. Inside, tiny young salmon are developing, but you wouldn't know it to look at them. Not yet.

Many of the forest's mammals—big, small and in-between—have retreated to dens, dams or burrows. Some, like squirrels, beavers, marmots and mice, are hibernating. They've fallen into an almost lifeless stupor. Their heart rates have slowed and their body temperatures have dropped, so if you tried to wake them, it would be like trying to wake the dead. The bears of the Great Bear Rainforest are also asleep but, unlike true hibernators, their body temperatures have dropped only slightly and their heart rates have hardly slowed. Instead, they've gone into a state scientists call *torpor*, which is a temporary sleep from which they can wake at any time. In fact, they often do. They get up, stretch their limbs and even go outside if the snow over their den doors isn't too deep and heavy. Sometimes, if there's a late run

of salmon in December, they'll go fishing. But this is rare. For the most part, the rainforest in winter is a place of wolves and deer.

However, winter in the Great Bear Rainforest is hard on both species, especially when they're old, weak or sick. Such animals often don't live to see another spring. Near the sea it doesn't snow too much, but farther inland and especially in the mountains, snow packs can be deep. In some places it can snow more than three meters (almost ten feet), making travel an exhausting challenge for deer or moose with their spindly, stiltlike legs.

In the deepest part of the forest, where the trees are tallest and thickest, animals can find shelter. The evergreen branches that spread in every direction act like umbrellas. You'll know that if you've ever run under a tree to escape the rain. In the rainforest, trees provide the same kind of shelter from snow. Even though there's snow on the branches, at the base of the tree very little will fall to the ground. This makes the biggest rainforest trees a good place for deer in winter because it's one of the few places where plants can still grow. In other words, thanks to these tree umbrellas, deer still have something to browse and nibble on.

This also illustrates the problem with clear-cutting a rainforest. Some people say that when a forest is logged, berry bushes will grow in place of the trees, and the more berry bushes there are, the more food there will be for animals such as deer. But that's only true for a short period of time and before snow has

WOLF BITES

Trees of the Great Bear Rainforest. The most common are the Sitka spruce, red cedar, western hemlock, amabilis fir and, farther south, the Douglas fir. The oldest trees in the GBR are more than 1,500 years old. The reason the forest is so rich in plant life, or biomass, is the cooler temperature. In tropical rainforests everything decomposes very quickly, but in the Great Bear Rainforest a fallen tree takes hundreds of years to decompose. Also, forests such as the GBR are so wet that they rarely suffer such disturbances as fires.

LEFT: **While bears and other rainforest animals spend the winter asleep, wolves are active all year long. Winters can be beautiful in the rainforest, but the harsh climate can also be hard on wolves.**

WOLF BITES

What makes the Great Bear Rainforest special?

The GBR is what's known as a coastal temperate rainforest—one of the rarest and most endangered forest types on Earth. A few hundred years ago such forests covered one-fifth of 1 percent of its surface. Since then more than 60 percent of them have been destroyed by industry and to make way for people. Coastal temperate forests have four distinguishing features: they exist in cooler climates; they're close to oceans; they're near mountains; and they get lots of rain. In addition to the Great Bear Rainforest, such forests can still be found in Alaska, portions of New Zealand, Tasmania, Chile and Argentina as well as in extremely limited parts of Japan, northwest Europe, and along the Black Sea in Turkey and the Republic of Georgia.

accumulated. When snow is deep on the ground, deer will die without a place to shelter. So if too many trees are logged, deer will have no place to go when old man winter gets brutal.

Winter also means storms. You now know that a good part of the Great Bear Rainforest is by the sea, and in winter, storms roll in from the Pacific like cannon balls. A big storm can hammer away at the trees and beaches for days. Trees blow over, raindrops feel like bullets, waves crash like cars, and the wind roars like a T. rex. It's dark too. On December 21, the northern hemisphere's shortest day, there isn't much more than a blink of daylight in the Great Bear Rainforest. Around Christmas and into January and February, there can be days when, as the old saying goes, "it ain't fit out for man or beast."

But animals like wolves and deer have no choice but to be out. They have to make their way in the rainforest no matter the time of year or the weather. For wolf pups, the arrival of winter means the lazy, pampered days of summer are gone, and for the first time in their short lives they have to travel with the full pack on hunts. At eight months old, a coastal wolf pup is almost as big as his or her parents, and at ten months, most are physically able to reproduce. So even though they're not yet a full year old, they're now an essential part of their families. And just as in human families, the wolf pack's future depends on their meeting responsibilities. When pups are small and helpless, older members of the pack will dote on them and present them with food in the same way human parents feed and dote on

their babies. But think about what happens when human babies get older. They're expected to take on duties and jobs. First it's school. Then it's chores like making beds and doing dishes. Then it's earning a living. The same thing happens in a wolf family. It just happens a lot faster.

In winter, even with the help of the now bigger, stronger pups, finding food is more difficult than at any other time of the year. The sea is still a source of sustenance—especially if a whale or sea lion carcass washes up on shore—but mainly it's the large hoofed animals of the rainforest—the deer, moose and mountain goats—that comprise most of a mainland wolf's winter diet. Island wolves depend on deer, mink, river otter and sea creatures.

TOP: **The weather in the Great Bear Rainforest is always changing. It can be sunny one day, rainy the next and stormy the day after that. In winter, storms can blow in with such force that full-grown trees topple over.**

WOLF BITES

How many different species of animals live in the Great Bear Rainforest?

About 350 bird and animal species have been identified so far. But it's impossible to know how many species of insects, spiders and soil organisms may live in the forest too. There could be tens of thousands of them.

RIGHT: **Wolves were once here, and these tracks prove it. Deer are the main prey item for rainforest wolves in winter, but catching them is seldom easy. Wolves know deer can't walk in deep snow, so a deer's best defense is to hide in the part of the rainforest where the snow isn't too deep. That's usually close to the coast.**

Catching and bringing down these animals is never easy. And it's doubly hard in winter. Which is why wolves usually go after older, sickly animals. A large healthy buck or moose can pack a deadly wallop with its hind hooves. An old or sick one no longer has the same kind of kick.

Also, because there are fewer prey animals in winter, wolf families often have to go farther to find them. In spring and summer, with so many smaller animals like beavers and martens around, wolves may use only a small portion of their territories to search for food. In winter, when there are only deer and moose left, they're likely to use all of it. But that takes energy, and energy requires fuel. And fuel requires food. So it's a vicious cycle. No wonder winter is often the last season old or sick wolves ever see.

As tough as winter is, it's also the season when wolves create new life. Pups are born in spring, but they're conceived near the end of winter. Each year, older, bolder members of a wolf family may try to earn the right to reproduce by challenging the alpha male and female. If the pack leaders are growing old or getting weak, these challenges might succeed. No one can be a leader forever. Otherwise the alpha male and female will hold on to their positions and become parents-to-be again. And sixty-three days later—usually it's as regular as clockwork—the female will give birth to a new litter of pups. However, mating time is also when some wolves may choose to leave the protection and familiarity of their families and strike out on their own either to start a new family in a different part of the coast

or to join another family in need of a new leader. This is how new wolf families are established. Just as young human adults long to leave their homes and live independently, so do some wolves.

This is life in the Great Bear Rainforest: always changing yet always enduring. The wolves who live there today aren't the same wolves who lived there twenty, fifty or a hundred years ago, but they're living lives very similar to those of all the wolves who came before them. Wolf pups learn from their parents. Then, when they're old enough to have pups of their own, they teach those pups. It's the never-ending cycle of life.

This book has described some of the similarities between wolves and people. But there's a very profound and significant difference too. For people, life rarely stays the same. Advances in technology consistently allow us to do things we couldn't do before. We fly all over the world, we communicate with each other instantaneously, and we gather dinner from every corner of the globe. When you open your fridge, you likely will find fresh food in it that came from any number of different countries. This is something your great-grandparents never would have dreamed was possible. By contrast, the lives coastal wolves live today are very much like the lives their great-grandparents lived—and even the lives their great-great-great-grandparents lived. Of course, wolves have to deal with natural changes. Some springs are kinder than others. Some winters are harsher. But through it all and no matter the challenges they face, the wolves of the Great Bear Rainforest endure—proud, precious and, above all, wild.

WOLF BITES

How fast can a wolf run?
Like people, wolves can only run really fast for a short period of time. Normally, they lope along at about 8 kilometers (5 miles) an hour, but when they're chasing a deer or a moose, they can run almost eight times that fast. Depending on where they live and the size of their territories, some wolves can travel as far as 80 kilometers (50 miles) a day searching for food. That's a long way, but with their inward-facing elbows, long legs and large bedroom-slipper paws, they can travel long distances without wasting a lot of energy.

LEFT: **Winter can be spectacular in the Great Bear Rainforest, but brutal too. It's the time of year when old and sick animals, including wolves, are most likely to die.**

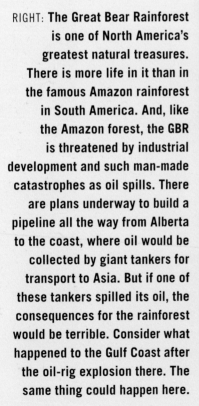

RIGHT: **The Great Bear Rainforest is one of North America's greatest natural treasures. There is more life in it than in the famous Amazon rainforest in South America. And, like the Amazon forest, the GBR is threatened by industrial development and such man-made catastrophes as oil spills. There are plans underway to build a pipeline all the way from Alberta to the coast, where oil would be collected by giant tankers for transport to Asia. But if one of these tankers spilled its oil, the consequences for the rainforest would be terrible. Consider what happened to the Gulf Coast after the oil-rig explosion there. The same thing could happen here.**

CHAPTER SEVEN

Friends in High Places

This book began by talking about how wolves have been feared and persecuted by people almost everywhere the two live side by side—which unfortunately is almost everywhere in the wolf's world. But not in the Great Bear Rainforest. The GBR has been home to different First Nations people for millennia—thousands of years. And far from making an enemy of the wolf, coastal First Nations have honored and respected it.

Before European explorers began colonizing British Columbia, the Great Bear Rainforest was home to tens of thousands of aboriginal people. But the way those people lived was very different from the way people live today. They relied on the forest and the ocean for everything. They ate fish,

LEFT: **One of the most curious friendships in the rainforest is between the wolf and the raven. Wolves have been documented eating all kinds of rainforest birds, but they've never been known to hunt or eat a raven.**

WOLF BITES

First Nations people in the Great Bear Rainforest.

Many different First Nation communities are found throughout the northern Great Bear Rainforest. Each continues to live in the same traditional territories that have supported their cultures for over ten thousand years. They include the Nuxalk, Gitga'at , Kitasoo-Xaixais, Heiltsuk, Wuikinuxv, Haisla, Tlingit and Metlakatla.

RIGHT: **Wolves and ravens share a long and mutually beneficial history. Ravens help wolves locate prey, and wolves help bite into the carcasses of animals whose skins are too tough for raven bills to penetrate.**

and they built their houses and crafted their canoes from the rainforest trees. They clothed themselves with skins from the animals they hunted and bark from the red cedar. Yes, they took from the forest but never more than what they needed to survive. They understood that nature was a balance, and that if that balance was tipped too far in one direction or the other, nature would suffer—and they would suffer too. It was their world, and they were part of it.

So it shouldn't come as a surprise to learn that just as the territories of wolves, bears and deer overlap each other in the Great Bear Rainforest today, so did the territories of animals and the villages of people hundreds of years ago. Life wasn't a competition between them the way it is now. There were no wire fences, garbage dumps and paved roads keeping people in and animals out. The villages Native people lived in fit into the forest like a bear or wolf den. In fact, many of the wolf dens that have been identified in the Great Bear Rainforest are near what were once First Nations village sites. BC coastal First Nations didn't drive wolves away or slaughter them as so many Europeans and North American settlers did; they lived next door to them. And they did so peaceably. First Nations people viewed the wolf as an intelligent, social and spiritually important animal. One only has to look at the carvings of wolves in their totems or the corner posts holding up their big house roofs to realize that the wolf was a culturally significant animal. Today, stories are still told that describe the wolf as a provider and protector.

TOP: **According to one First Nation legend, the raven created the rainforest by dropping pebbles into the sea. These turned into islands, providing a home for other rainforest animals like this spirit bear.**

But it's not only coastal people who have had a close relationship with coastal wolves. Strange as it may sound, ravens and wolves have long been good rainforest friends, and they remain so today. Sometimes when you see a flock of ravens traveling through the forest, a family of wolves won't be far away. And while coastal wolves will eat almost any bird they manage to catch—herons, geese, cranes, ducks, you name it—they aren't known to eat ravens.

If you've never seen a raven, they look very much like the common crow, only bigger. The best way to tell the two apart is to look at their tail feathers. The raven's form a wedge, while the crow's are blocked off in kind of a square. Ravens are excellent fliers. They can soar hundreds of meters above the ground and travel great distances in a single day—as much as sixty-five kilometers (forty miles). They also can perform amazing acrobatics in the sky—dive-bombing and looping the loop—and have a very elaborate language. Sometimes they sound like falling water or a cat meowing. They can even imitate human language.

The raven is famous in some Pacific First Nations cultures for being the creator of the world. According to one legend, Raven created land when he grew tired of flying over an open ocean—the Pacific. He dropped pebbles into the sea that grew into the islands off what is now the BC coast. Then, using wood and clay, he made animals and humans so the islands wouldn't be empty. This explains why the raven, like the wolf, figures so prominently in First Nations carvings and artwork.

To coastal wolves, however, the raven is important for more practical reasons. If a seal or a whale happens to wash up on the opposite side of an island, the wolves may not know about it right away. But the ravens will because they can see a lot more from the air than wolves do from the ground. So the ravens will call the wolves and tell them about the carcass. Why? Not because ravens are especially generous. In nature, creatures rarely are. Usually when they do something, they do it for themselves. In this case, deer, moose, seal and sea lion skin is tough—too tough for a raven to break open on its own. So if there's a family of wolves willing to do it for them, why not let them? For ravens it's like having their own crew of butchers. The only catch is that these butchers usually want their share of the meat first.

WOLF BITES

Wolves and First Nations.

Every First Nation in the Great Bear Rainforest owns stories that describe what wolves mean to its culture. Some, like the Heiltsuk people in Bella Bella, describe the wolf as a protector in one of their creation stories. The Nuxalk Nation describes wolves as sacred and says wolves and humans can be transformed into one another. In one Nuxalk story, a woman who saved a wolf by removing a bone from its throat was in turn granted special healing powers by the wolf as a reward. The Gitga'at people from Hartley Bay also describe wolves as having special hunting powers and say these powers enable them to transform into humans. One of the unifying themes among First Nations on the coast is that wolves are part of their culture and are respected, not feared or persecuted.

WOLF BITES

Wolves around the world.

Scientists recognize three distinct species of wolves in the world. They are the gray wolf, the red wolf and the Ethiopian wolf, though some scientists now believe the Ethiopian wolf is more jackal than wolf. There are five subspecies, or races, of gray wolves. They are the Mexican wolf, the Great Plains or buffalo wolf, the Rocky Mountain wolf, the eastern timber wolf and the arctic wolf. However, now scientists believe it's time to add the BC coastal wolf to that list. Significant populations of gray wolves continue to live in Canada, Alaska and Russia. Small populations can also be found in east Africa, southern Asia, Europe and a few of the forty-eight contiguous states, including Montana, Idaho and Wyoming.

Ravens also alert wolves to intruders and help keep the places wolves live clean. They're excellent scavengers, so they eat whatever scraps wolves leave behind. And even though this sounds gross, ravens will eat wolf droppings because there's nutritious stuff in them. For example, when a wolf eats a seal carcass, not everything gets digested as it passes through the wolf's gut. So a raven can benefit when it eats what's politely known as wolf "scat."

However, the relationship between wolves and ravens is about more than just food. It's also about fun. If you have a pet, you'll know that animals love to play. Wild animals do too. The same Pacific First Nations who credit the raven with creating the world also credit him as a trickster. No one in the forest is said to like a game or joke better than a raven. So sometimes ravens and wolves play tag. They chase each other like children across the broad stretches of island sand. Other times ravens dive-bomb wolf pups like kamikaze pilots and then nip at their ears as they take off again. It drives the leaping pups crazy. Or if they don't attack the pups from the air, they may act like hunting decoys on the ground. They walk in front of the pups and the pups stalk them as if they were stalking deer. But the wily raven is too clever to be caught. Just when the pup is about to pounce, the raven will fly away. This curiously endearing relationship is played out everywhere wolves and ravens exist together.

Members of the Tlingit First Nation, who live in the northernmost part of the Great Bear Rainforest, have observed this close wolf-raven relationship for

centuries. In fact, the wolf and the raven have become major symbols in their culture. Every member of the Tlingit Nation belongs to either the wolf or the raven clan. Clan membership is determined by one's mother. If your mother is a raven, you'll be a raven too. If she is a wolf, you'll be a wolf. According to Tlingit custom, those from the wolf clan are only allowed to marry someone from the raven clan, and ravens are only allowed to marry wolves. As well, a member of one clan must perform funeral rites for a member of the other clan. And at feast time, only wolves may serve ravens (and vice versa).

So, who's afraid of the big bad wolf? Certainly not people who understand them. For millennia, it must have seemed to the Tlingit and other coastal

TOP: **While European cultures have historically despised the wolf and most often hunted it to near extinction, First Nations cultures have always honored it. Here a group of Heiltsuk youth celebrates wolves and wolf culture at a big house.**

First Nations that the rainforest belonged to them and the animals. They lived side by side as the seasons changed and the years passed. Then something happened. Two hundred and fifty years ago, European explorers set eyes on the beautiful BC coast, and nothing has been the same since. As European and, later, Asian cultures and customs overtook those of First Nations people as the preeminent cultures of British Columbia, the rainforest changed too. Industry arrived. Trees were cut. Animals were shot for sport, and rivers were polluted and emptied of fish. Explorers brought modern ways to the rainforest, and while those modern ways have brought an economic advantage to many, it has come at a terrible cost to the natural world.

WOLF BITES

What fish other than salmon do coastal wolves eat?

Herring. In March, huge schools of these small silvery fish swim into the shallow waters of the Great Bear Rainforest to lay what to wolves are tasty fat white eggs. These eggs attach themselves to seaweed on the rocky shores, so at low tide wolves lick them off in mouthfuls of a hundred or more. They're just one more food item the bounteous ocean provides rainforest wolves.

LEFT: **First Nations people living along the BC coast pay their respects to wolves by wearing their skins and creating masks in their likeness.**

RIGHT: **A wolf and three ravens share a misty gray day on the coast.**

RIGHT: **The relationship between ravens and wolves isn't always about work. Sometimes it's about play. The raven is known by coastal First Nations as the trickster of the rainforest. No wonder. Wolves and ravens will play tag with each other, and ravens will tease wolf pups by dive-bombing them like kamikaze pilots and nipping at their ears as they take off again. This drives the leaping, yelping pups crazy, but the ravens don't care. They're enjoying themselves too much.**

CHAPTER EIGHT

Into the Future

Today the future of the Great Bear Rainforest—and the future of the wolves who inhabit it—is more uncertain than it's ever been. Unfortunately, the same is true for many of the world's wild animals these days. After tens of thousands of years enjoying a fairly predictable and secure environment, the rainforest is changing quickly and irrevocably due to the encroachment of people and the spread of industry.

In recent years some progress has been made to safeguard the coastal wolf and other wildlife in the Great Bear Rainforest. About 30 percent of the total land area of the GBR is now protected from logging, and while this certainly is a step in the right direction, scientists hired by the government to study the area say at least 70 percent needs to

LEFT: **BC's Great Bear Rainforest is as breathtaking as it is endangered. The forest's future is now a precarious one, mostly due to human greed.**

WOLF BITES

What will save our salmon for the future?

Fisheries officials need to recognize that more creatures than just people eat salmon. Currently, when these officials determine how many salmon commercial and sport fishermen may catch each year, they don't take into account the tens of thousands of rainforest animals who rely on salmon too. Conservationists believe this need should be an important consideration when officials decide how many salmon it's safe for people to catch.

be protected if its wildlife, including wolves, is to be safe over the long term. So more needs to be done. Part of the problem is that much of the 30 percent now protected is made up of land where the animals don't actually live. Much of it is rock and ice (mountains and glaciers), and not enough of it is composed of the forest where wolves, deer and moose spend most of their time.

Other issues threaten the long-term survival of rainforest wolves too. Although people don't eat wolf meat, they continue to kill them for sport, for their fur and out of fear. Wolves receive almost no special protection from BC hunting regulations. They may even be hunted within the new conservancies and parks inside the GBR. Consequently, much more needs to be done to convince the government to protect these intelligent social creatures.

Even if people were to stop killing wolves, there is still the question of whether there will always

RIGHT: **For thousands of years BC's coastal wolves have lived in relative peace. No more. Now they're being threatened on all sides by hunting, trapping and industry. Their future, as never before, is in our hands.**

LEFT: **Road building and clear-cut logging are harmful to wolves because they destroy the forest the wolves live in, and they make it easier for hunters and trappers to gain access to wild wolves.**

be enough for them to eat. You now know how vital salmon are to coastal wolves. During the fall, salmon are their most important source of nutrition. But what if there were no more salmon? That's not as far-fetched a fear as you might think. In recent years the Canadian government has done a terrible job managing fish stocks on both the east and west coasts of the country. Year after year scientists point to rivers where, according to government predictions, millions of salmon were forecast to return in the fall. Instead only a fraction of the fish show up. Why? Even our best scientists don't fully understand the complex issues facing migrating salmon. There is, however, a great deal of evidence to suggest that overfishing, fish farms and climate change have all played a role in their decline. The BC government has said it won't allow any more fish farms to be built along the northern coast of the Great Bear Rainforest, but they continue to operate and expand farther south. And thanks to climate change, the world's oceans are getting warmer. Salmon are sensitive to even slight changes in temperature, so what if it gets too warm for them in the north Pacific?

There is also talk of building an oil-tanker port on BC's north coast, possibly in Kitimat, in the very heart of the Great Bear Rainforest. Industry and government are looking for a more efficient way to transport oil and natural gas from Alberta and northeastern BC to the coast, where it can be shipped to other countries. As well, some people would like to see offshore drilling stations built along the forest's coast, since it's believed rich deposits of oil

WOLF BITES

The pipeline issue.

The proposed pipeline would reach from northern Alberta, where the oil is pumped from the ground, to the town of Kitimat on the BC coast. Oil is very much in demand in Asian countries, and such a pipeline would make it easier for Canada to ship oil to Asia. But what of the risks involved? Allowing huge oil tankers to collect crude oil from a pipeline in this sensitive and important ecological area could have devastating consequences if a tanker were to spring a leak, run aground or sink. Even now, more than 20 years after the *Exxon Valdez* oil disaster, scientists continue to discover long-term harmful impacts on the environment.

LEFT: **The pristine waters that wolves enjoy off the coast of the Great Bear Rainforest would be destroyed if an oil tanker were to run aground and spill its contents the way the *Exxon Valdez* did in 1989 in Alaska.**

WOLF BITES

Climate change and the rainforest.
Scientists are concerned that because salmon are so sensitive to temperature changes, a warmer ocean could mean that these fish won't survive long enough to reproduce. They also worry that warmer rivers and streams might cause salmon eggs to hatch too soon. Finally, they say climate change could increase the severity and frequency of winter floods and summer droughts. Both these extreme weather changes could seriously endanger salmon populations.

RIGHT: **For thousands of years coastal wolves have enjoyed a forest home where they've been safe from human encroachment. Now that's starting to change.**

are buried there. If that happens, there's no telling what the consequences might be.

In 1989, a tanker named the *Exxon Valdez* ran aground off the coast of Alaska and spilled almost 42 million liters (11 million gallons) of crude oil into the sea, killing thousands of marine mammals (seals, whales, otters, sea lions) and birds in the process. Until recently this was the worst oil spill in North American history. Then on April 20, 2010, a British Petroleum oil rig called the Deepwater Horizon exploded in the Gulf of Mexico, killing eleven and injuring seventeen workers, and allowing more than 750,000 liters (200,000 gallons) of oil to spill into the sea every day. By the time the well was plugged (late July 2010), as many as 640 million liters (170 million gallons) of oil had gushed into the surrounding ocean. That's enough oil to fill half the Empire State Building. The environmental damage from this spill has yet to be assessed, but there is little doubt that it will affect the Gulf Coast for years.

Even after such catastrophic disasters as these, some people continue to insist that oil drilling at sea is a good thing. There is no doubt that similar disasters could and most likely would eventually occur if an oil port or offshore drilling stations were built near the Great Bear Rainforest. Imagine what would happen to its rivers and beaches.

Nevertheless, in spite of all these dangers, we have to believe that, as long as coastal wolves live in the rainforest, and as long as people care about them, they will survive. After all, it wasn't that long ago that hardly anyone, aside from the First Nations people

who share the land with them, knew what amazing animals these wolves are. That's changed. As more and more people the world over have learned about this astonishing piece of wilderness and the fascinating animals that inhabit it, more and more want it and them protected.

So as you can now see, wolves—and particularly coastal wolves—aren't big and bad in the way so many stories say. In some ways they're as fragile as great art. As precious too. They are uniquely noble symbols of what once was a truly wild Earth—an Earth that exists now in only a few places like the Great Bear Rainforest. Everyone wants to leave a better world for his or her children. Well, imagine a world without the rainforest and the fascinating creatures who call it home. Think what a sad and empty world that would be. But unless we change our greedy, short-sighted ways, it's the kind of world we'll be leaving our children and their children. And the coastal wolves? If we don't take real steps to safeguard them and the great green forest in which they roam, the only places where they'll remain will be in stories and books— like this one.

WOLF BITES

Endangered populations.

Wolves used to live in Mexico too, but they have since been wiped out. Now the Mexican wolf lives in Arizona and New Mexico, where only about fifty individual animals still roam free. A few hundred more survive in captivity. The red wolf is also almost extinct. There are only about one hundred or so individual animals left. They live in southeast Texas, southwest Louisiana and a small part of North Carolina, where they were reintroduced recently by conservationists. The eastern Canadian red wolf is a close cousin of the American red wolf and is also critically endangered. Small numbers exist in Algonquin Provincial Park in Ontario and east over the Quebec border.

LEFT: **Who's to say what the future of BC's coastal wolves will be? Will they even have a future? That's up to people to decide.**

FOR MORE INFORMATION

The wolves of the Great Bear Rainforest need your help. Trophy hunting, diminishing salmon stocks, habitat loss and oil spills threaten these magnificent animals.

Pacific Wild is a non-profit wildlife conservation organization that is committed to protecting the wolves in the Great Bear Rainforest by developing and implementing solution-based strategies that protect wildlife and their habitat. Pacific Wild has been at the forefront of large carnivore conservation on the British Columbia coast by supporting innovative research, public education, community outreach and awareness to achieve the goal of lasting wildlife protection. A portion of the royalties earned from the sale of this book will support Pacific Wild's work to protect wolves in the Great Bear Rainforest.

For more information on Pacific Wild's conservation work or to learn more about the wolves of the Great Bear Rainforest please contact:

Pacific Wild
PO Box 26
Denny Island, BC
V0T 1B0
Canada

WEBSITE: www.pacificwild.org
EMAIL: info@pacificwild.org

OTHER SUGGESTED READING

Busch, Robert H. *The Wolf Almanac*, 2nd ed. Guilford, CT:
The Lyons Press, 1998.

McAllister, Ian. *The Last Wild Wolves: Ghosts of the Rainforest*.
Vancouver: Greystone Books, 2007.

Mech, L. David. *The Wolf: The Ecology and Behavior of an Endangered
Species*. Minneapolis: University of Minnesota Press, 1981.

ABOUT THE ARTIST

An artist from childhood, Martin Campbell depicts scenes of his daily life
and Heiltsuk culture in his work.

INDEX

Page numbers in **bold** refer to photographs.